COUNTDOWN TO COLLEGE:

Preparing Your Student For Success In The Collegiate Universe

...the 40 tips you'll want to know beforehand.

This parents'survival manual is written for every parent who is worried about sending his or her student away to college. It is a "must have" guide that prepares you to deal with the inevitable trials and conflicts that come with making the college transition.

Countdown to College:
Preparing Your Student For Success
In The Collegiate Universe

Published by:
BLUE BIRD PUBLISHING

2266 S. Dobson, Suite #275
Mesa AZ 85202
(602) 831-6063 FAX (602) 831-1829
Email: bluebird@bluebird1.com
Web site: http://www.bluebird1.com

Printed in the United States of America
ISBN 0-933025- 55-6
Cover Design by Joe Hansen
Cover Illustration by Cori Zeller & Will Nelson

Library of Congress Cataloging-in-Publication Data

Anderson, Shawn L., 1962-
  Countdown to college : preparing your student for
success in the collegiate universe : the 40 tips you'll want
to know beforehand / [Shawn L. Anderson].
      p. cm.
  ISBN 0-933025-55-6
  1. College student orientation--United States. 2. College
  students--United States--Conduct of Life. 3. College
  Students--United States--Family relationships. I. Title.
  LB2343.32.A53   197
  378'.198--dc21   97-1671
                                                       CIP

To All Parents
who care about their child's success
and who remember just how much fun
...and stressful...
college can be.

<u>CONTENTS</u>

A time to build...career.

A time to experience...campus life.

A time to learn...academics.

A time to prepare...situations of conflict.

A time to support...family changes.

March....April...May...June... July...August...September. The countdown to college.

If you have a son or daughter preparing for college, the final countdown has begun. Whether it's months, weeks, or even days until the fall semester begins, your life and your college bound student's life will soon change.

With one fewer person at home competing for phone time and bathroom time, you will experience a multitude of different emotions. You will also experience a variety of new situations in which your college student will require your help.

This guide, *COUNTDOWN TO COLLEGE: Preparing Your Student For Success In The Collegiate Universe ...the 40 tips you'll want to know beforehand,* is written for parents who are concerned about sending their son or daughter away to school. It is a "must have" manual that prepares you to deal with the inevitable trials and conflicts that come with making the college transition.

For most families, the process that has led up to your son or daughter actually leaving for college has probably been somewhat melodramatic. Waking up late on SAT Saturday...debating over where to apply...cramming to get the applications in before the deadline...opening the acceptance or denial envelopes...there is no doubt that preparing to get

8

your teenager off to college has certainly been an emotional roller coaster.

Unfortunately, the ride does not end once college begins.

Regardless of how solid your son or daughter's future plans seem to be, most students struggle with adjusting to the new environment. Additionally, the new found autonomy and independence that a first year student experiences is bound to cause some freshman to make a few poor decisions. And although learning from these mistakes is part of the maturing process for your student, it is important to be nearby with an encouraging word and a few answers that can help get your student back on track.

This book will give you the inside scoop on what to expect. Some of the ideas represented in the 40 section headings will serve as red flags to watch out for, while other ideas will help clarify your thoughts and, perhaps, stimulate solutions to difficult scenarios. Whichever the case, this valuable resource guide will help you focus your thinking and plan your actions.

Common sense is not common knowledge. Even the best parents can be caught off guard by their freshman's actions. *COUNTDOWN TO COLLEGE* addresses potential problems ranging from poor test scores to alcohol indulgence. It will help you with solutions. It will help your son or daughter with results.

I wish you success on your journey!
—Shawn L. Anderson

Foreword

As the Executive Director of the Educational Assistance Council, I have committed my career to helping students succeed at the collegiate level. For the past 18 years, the Council has helped thousands of families prepare for a son or daughter leaving for college both financially and academically. We are the college success experts.

Over the years, the Council has reviewed hundreds of texts on college planning—only one has earned the Council's endorsement. Shawn Anderson's *Countdown to College: Preparing Your Student For Success in the Collegiate Universe* is extremely thorough, clear and concise. If offers tremendous value in helping your son or daughter succeed in college, and it is the only collegiate success product that we have ever chosen to endorse outside of our own material.

Whether it be the stress associated with leaving home, the demanding rigors of college classes, or a lack of discipline handling new freedoms, college students adjust to the college transition differently. This book is all about helping them adjust successfully. It will be a terrific reference tool to guide your action when a particular situation arises.

I wholeheartedly recommend that you read *Countdown to College*. I take great pride in endorseing a book that I know will make a difference. It is good...very good.

—Dr. John W. Geranios, Executive Director
Educational Assistance Council, Inc.
Burbank, California

A time to build...career.

1. Majors:
helping choose a direction.

If your student is uncertain in choosing a major, don't worry. Do, however, *encourage your student to research viable options*. Although he/she might be apt to spend more time deciding which movie to see on Saturday, this is not an endeavor that should be confronted half-heartily.

Investing the necessary time and effort in choosing a major now can mean less frustration later. You know this. Your role in the "major" selection process is to convince your student of this also. Although many students have been known to change their major three, four, or even five times, you can help your student avoid this path by sharing the following suggestions:

1. Encourage self-assessment tests.
In determining a major, the self-assessment process is crucial. This first step is important for helping to pinpoint your student's interests and aptitudes. Your college bound freshman can ask his/her high school counselor for self-assessment information or check the library for a wide

range of books available on the topic.

Additionally, the Educational Assistance Council (Toll-free 800-852-8900) has developed a state of the art assessment test called the Career Guidance Report. By filling out an extensive interest inventory, your student will receive a personalized report that shows where his/her aptitudes lie.

2. Counselors, professionals, professors...ask them.

Encourage your freshman to *be as inquisitive as possible* as he/she selects a major. Again, the high school counseling office can be a key resource. A counselor can provide your student with material giving an overview of each prospective major.

Additionally, you should encourage your student to meet with professionals in the field. *There is no better way to discover whether or not a particular field is appealing than to talk to people who make a living from it.* Many professionals (and professors) would be happy to take the time to answer your son or daughter's questions.

3. Job market demand shouldn't be the #1 factor in choosing a major.

Just because the job market is "hot" for a particular major doesn't mean that your son or daughter should choose it. Your student will be much happier selecting a major in which he/she is genuinely interested. If your teenager is passionate about a specific major, encourage him/her to pursue it.

Although you may be nervous about your "financial investment" and concerned about your student's future, *avoid putting unnecessary pressure on your student to enter a major that might be popular with you.* Additionally, if your son or daughter is inclined to enroll in a liberal arts major, don't panic. The myth that a liberal arts major is unemployable is not true.

4. Consider a minor or a double major.

After taking the courses necessary to get into a major, your student might discover that more than one course of study is appealing. If that is the case, a minor or a double major should be strongly considered. Although the challenge of meeting the requirements for two majors will be more difficult, your student is certainly opening the door for a greater selection of career possibilities. *If your scholar has the motivation to accomplish the goal of achieving a double major, strongly encourage him/her.*

Words to pass on...

A goal (major) casually set and lightly taken is freely abandoned at the first obstacle.

2. Careers:
helping choose a future.

It is not uncommon for parents to push their kids to declare a career by the 8th grade. Ludicrous? Only when <u>other</u> moms and dads do it. Of course, we take great pride in announcing to our friends, "Michelle hasn't fully decided, but she's either going to be a doctor or a lawyer." Forget the fact that Michelle hasn't even taken the PSAT!

Establishing a career is something that comes with time. Sure, *it's important to choose a direction in life, but your teenager doesn't have to make a final decision in his/her freshman year.* What is important, however, is that your student begins to familiarize him/herself with options that he/she finds interesting.

It's great if your student has a career in mind (as long as it's his/her decision), but if your freshman doesn't, don't put pressure on him/her to choose now. Here are two practical steps that you can encourage instead:

1. Begin collecting information.
Research, evaluation, and more research are the keys to making an informed decision about career choice. *Strongly encourage your son or daughter to begin collecting in-*

formation about career opportunities and fields of interest. Articles and valuable data and statistics can be found in a variety of printed and computerized resources. Self-assessment tests can help to give your student's mission direction.

2. Encourage a first hand look.

As much as the first step will guide the mind, this step will guide the heart. *Experiencing the <u>realities</u> of a profession first-hand can really help your student decide whether or not a particular career has long-term potential.* Here are a few options that your student can investigate:

✳ Part-time jobs...

This is a terrific way to explore a career in which your student might be interested. A part-time job offers your freshman *the opportunity to gain valuable work experience and is often a key link in helping him/her make a career decision.* Part-time jobs can also be easier to create for a prospective employer.

✳ Internships...

In many internship programs, employers take the time to explain the ins-and-outs of the job and organization. Usually, your student has the chance to assist on an assignment that relates directly to his/her education and career aspiration. *Occasionally, your student will have to "sell" the internship idea to a desired employer.* There isn't a better way for your freshman to learn personal marketing skills.

✳ Volunteer...

Sometimes, the only way to hook up with a specific organization is to volunteer. Understandably, this isn't the most popular option. If, however, your student's purpose is to link up with a specific business, the fact that he/she is working for free isn't as important right now. The experience and insight that your student will receive from this opportunity can be invaluable in helping him/her get a foot in the door.

Words to pass on...

*Ask your student,
"If you could do anything in the world,
what would it be?"*

*"If you have built castles in the air,
your work need not be lost;
that is where they should be.
Now put foundations under them."
- Henry David Thoreau*

3. Jobs:
<u>*helping find employment while at school.*</u>

With the rising cost of college, your son or daughter may choose to work while going to school. *Either in an effort to help defray education expenses or to acquire spending money, many students are faced with the task of finding a job.* Here are a few places that you can suggest to your student in his/her search:

1. On campus...

Ranging from a popular job in the athletic department to a less attractive job serving meals in the dorm, competition for campus jobs varies a great deal. To many students, however, the need to pick up a check is more important than the nature of the work.

✶ See what is posted.

The campus employment office is a good place for your student to start looking for a job. Maybe he/she meets the requirements needed to apply for a position in the *work study program (on-campus and off-campus jobs coordinated through the financial aid office)*. If not, don't worry. Other good job openings will also be posted.

✳ **Look at home.**

If your student lives in the dorm, he/she might be able to find a job doing maintenance, custodial, security, cafeteria or mailroom work. A very popular position is working as a resident assistant (dorm administrator). Usually reserved for non-freshman, this job often provides discounts on room and board.

✳ **Be resourceful.**

It is also a good idea to contact campus departments directly. Maybe something in the athletic department doesn't pan out, but perhaps the Visitor's Center is looking for a tour guide. The most attractive positions are often not posted. Aggressive and resourceful job searches tend to uncover great jobs!

2. Off campus...

Recommend that your student check out the businesses around campus. Many of these businesses are employed solely by students and are subject to higher turnover (graduation, changing jobs, etc.), so finding a job is often easier. For students who live off campus and don't want to cook, working in a fraternity or sorority might be a good idea because job duties are often exchanged for meals.

3. Look ahead to summer...

Advise your student to apply for a summer position as soon as possible. Sending out resumes as early as the fall of the preceding year is an excellent idea. *Many terrific jobs are found through direct inquiries and not necessarily Help Wanted ads.*

Words to pass on...

*"**G**ive me a stock clerk with a goal,*
and I will give you a man who will make history.
Give me a man without a goal,
and I will give you a stock clerk."
- J.C. Penney

*T*o *get your foot in the door, you need to put*
your foot in the door.

4. Networking:
<u>*helping to develop contacts.*</u>

Networking is all about "growing" relationships. *Encouraging your son or daughter to develop contacts with key individuals at school can prove very advantageous in your student's future.* Not only are there short-term benefits (i.e., getting to know professors), but the potential long-term benefits (i.e., landing a job) can be invaluable!

Here are a few doors in which you should encourage your son or daughter to knock on beginning from day one:

1. Faculty members...

There are two significant benefits in networking with faculty members. First, by meeting with professors and teaching assistants, *your student will enhance the quality of his/her education.* By meeting one-on-one or in small groups, your student will have the opportunity to explore course information in greater depth. He/she will have the chance to ask questions and exchange ideas in a non-threatening environment.

Equally important, *your student will need letters of reference when he/she graduates* and needs to get a job or apply to

graduate school. Now is a terrific time to begin to cultivate faculty members who can write those future letters.

2. Campus staff...

It can also be advantageous for your student to network with
staff members at the student employment office. These
individuals can point out the most attractive job openings. *They can also help your student develop a resume
and provide valuable assistance in directing job searches.*

3. Employers...

*It is never too early to begin building a network of potential
employers,* either for a future career position or just a job
for the summer. After developing a list of conceivable
places that he/she would like to work (possibly with help
from a friend at the student employment office), your student should begin to make contact through resumes and
phone calls.

*Encourage your student to let prospective employers know
that he/she is interested in their organization.* Perhaps
your freshman can seek advice as to what skills the employer might be looking for in future employees. In his/
her correspondence, encourage your student to ask questions that solicit a response. In this way, he/she will have
developed a personal contact within the organization that
can be used to begin the networking process.

*By finding a hero within the organization, your student has
someone to potentially direct him/her to opportunities,* or
at the very least, to other people, within the company.
This might be a time consuming process, but it could be
the key to landing a very popular position with a dynamic
company.

21

Networking is an important tool that can create fantastic opportunities in life. The practice of simply letting certain individuals know that "I care about my education...my grades...my future" can be a very important exercise in getting your student noticed by people who can open doors for him/her.

Words to pass on...

N etworking is a contact sport.

"T here is no such thing as a self-made man.
You will reach your goals
only with the help of others."
- George Shinn

A lot of people have gone further than they
thought they could because someone else
thought that they could.

5. Resume building:
things that employers notice.

Melting one's life down into resume form usually represents a necessary step in the job hunting process. An attractive resume that is well written and organized definitely plays a role in creating a favorable impression in the mind of a prospective employer. However, the core of every resume, the meat and potatoes so to speak, are the details that illustrate your student's capabilities and experiences.

Here are a few areas that your student should focus on from the outset in his/her effort to build a resume that stimulates employer interest:

1. Grades...
Pure and simple, good grades stand out. Good grades can be an indication of intelligence, work ethic, resourcefulness, and the ability to achieve bottom line results. At school, *your student's top priority should be to get the best marks possible.*

2. Educational course work...
Many employers look for students who have done well in specific classes. Skill oriented careers, such as engineering or accounting, require a prospective employee to have a

background in certain subject areas. Make sure that your student is not eliminated from potential opportunities by taking all classes necessary.

3. Work experience...

In their search for top job candidates, *employers will look at past work experience very closely.* Encourage your student to take advantage of summer breaks by seeking out positions and internships that can provide key experience and training.

4. Communication skills...

Some employers consider the ability to communicate the most valuable skill a student can learn in college. Being able to confidently communicate an idea is critical in many positions. Your student should look into adding a variety of writing, rhetoric, communication, education, and psychology courses to his/her academic schedule.

5. Leadership potential...

Organizational success centers on a company's ability to recognize and grow leaders. *Demonstrated leadership skills such as the ability to direct group activity and motivate others can make the difference in the hiring process.* Your student can assure high marks in this area by leading campus activities and clubs.

6. Extra-curricular activities...

Students who have been involved in activities outside of class often find themselves to be popular after graduation with employers. *Well-rounded students are those who have done more than study.* It's true that certain graduate schools (such as medical schools) don't consider this a top priority, but any student looking for a job immediately upon graduation should consider being involved in extra-curricular activities. Encourage your student to become involved.

The facts that bare out what your student has accomplished are critical in determining whether or not an employer is interested. Achievements and experiences are gauges that can determine future success. Instead of debating this rule of thumb, it makes more sense to live up to it. Encourage your student to take an active interest in developing a resume that employers will notice.

Words to pass on...

*T**he only way to reach long-range goals
is through achieving short-range objectives.*

A time to experience...campus life.

6. Feeling comfortable:
<u>getting oriented to college.</u>

For many college-bound teenagers, making the transition from the comforts of home and the security of close friends to an unknown environment can be intimidating. For some, the change is as dramatic as changes come.

From mom's cooking to dorm food, from a room that he/she grew up in to a vacant apartment with wallpaper peeling and nail holes everywhere, the first few days of college are emotional. For those leaving home for school, this is one 24 hour period that has the potential to be a Twilight Zone episode.

Regardless of all the parenting mistakes that you're now feeling guilty about, this is your chance to go down in the record books as a terrific parent. Do everything that you can to help make your son or daughter's transition as smooth as possible. *Spend time talking through concerns. Ask questions. Listen. Keep everything positive and be a motivator.*

Here are a few other things that you can do to help your student feel more comfortable about heading off to college:

Countdown to College

1. Getting oriented academically...

* Read everything that comes in the mail.

Encourage your son or daughter to read everything that the college sends (you should read it, too!). *Make sure that your student understands the ins-and-outs of class registration and has put ample thought into choosing a first semester schedule.* Also, it's important to have a few back-up classes in case the first choices are filled.

* Link up with other students.

If your student is nervous about college, *arrange a meeting with a student who previously attended the same high school* and is now a year or two ahead in college. This meeting offers your student the chance to talk with somebody who has the same educational background and who is succeeding at the next academic level. Sharing fears with someone who has gone down the same path already can be very helpful.

2. Getting oriented socially...

* Get to know people early.

Arranging meetings with current students also helps in the area of social orientation. Certainly, knowing somebody before entering a new environment can be quite a relief. Do your best to help make these meetings possible.

* Attend orientation.

A terrific way for your son or daughter to develop a network of friends before school even starts is to attend freshman orientation. By avoiding orientation, your student is missing a valuable opportunity to start building confidence. Usually conducted in a very positive and friendly atmosphere, orientation is a time where questions are answered and shaky nerves are calmed. *Orientation is definitely a "can't miss" event.*

If you do attend orientation with your student, *purchase a student activity card* for him/her. This is a gesture that will be very much appreciated as it gives your son or daughter the opportunity to attend games and events with other students.

✶ **Get involved immediately.**

If there is a particular club or organization that your student is interested in joining, encourage him/her to contact the leader. Perhaps your student will have the chance to be a part of an orientation activity, and at the very least, your student will learn what the early schedule of events will be. *Early participation can definitely help your student feel a part of things.*

3. Getting oriented physically...

✶ **Visit the campus.**

The size and layout of some college campuses can be intimidating. This feeling can be overcome by visiting the campus and walking every inch of it. Encourage your student to tour departmental buildings, the student center, the book store, dorms, fraternities and sororities, the student employment center, the library, and other administrative buildings. *Tour everything.* Familiarity breeds confidence.

✶ **Accompany your student on the first visit.**

If your student is going to be attending college a considerable distance from home, it is recommended that you *take the trip with him/her when he/she heads out to school.* Even if the trip is going to be expensive, make the effort.

Countdown to College

Going the "extra mile" and being there with your student can make a difference in helping him/her adjust to the new changes. This helps you, too. Not only do you become more comfortable with where your student is heading, but you have the opportunity to create some great memories.

A final note...

When school does start, *call a few times the first week.* Your confidence and reassuring voice can help balance out some of the early trials that your student might be experiencing. If things are going well, it will give you the chance to share in your freshman's excitement.

Words to pass on...

"*T* *he little reed, bending to the force of the wind, soon stood upright again when the storm had passed over."*
- Aesop

7. Activities:

helping your son/daughter get involved in campus activities.

Attending college can be one of life's unique and memorable adventures. Usually, however, the treasured memories that still make us smile have little to do with late nights at the library. Great memories were more than likely centered on time spent with friends or with people who were fighting for the same causes. It was those fun and significant experiences that made the preparation for finals palatable. It still is.

Being involved and contributing to an organization establishes purpose and allows your student the opportunity to develop important interactive skills. With so many options, it is likely that at least one or two organizations will strike a passionate chord. For parents who are interested in helping their student become involved, here are a few suggestions:

1. Make good use of the summer before school starts.

Far too many students fail to take advantage of the first summer before school starts. This short hiatus before your student has to "buckle down and get serious" (an expression that is popular by parents of college bound freshman) is the perfect time to inquire about the different clubs and activities the campus has to offer.

Maybe your college-bound freshman is excited about joining a political organization or professional association. Encourage your student to take the initiative and make contact with the group during the summer. *This strategy could be particularly valuable in regard to rushing a fraternity or sorority.* Knowing someone in the house before Greek Rush starts could pay off in meeting other members of the house later.

2. For fun...follow the crowd.

One of the best ways for your student to get to know other people from his/her dorm or class is to purchase a student activity card. Football and basketball games at many college campuses are a must...even for those who didn't like attending these events in high school. By encouraging your student to attend the games, you are encouraging the opportunity for your son or daughter to develop relationships.

3. If it doesn't exist...start it.

If the organization in which your student is interested in participating doesn't exist, challenge your student to start one. Certainly, there must be other students who have the same desire. *Posting flyers around campus and putting an ad in the school paper can help drum up other students with the same passion.*

31

<u>*Words to pass on...*</u>

"Your problem is to bridge the gap which exists
between where you are now and the goal
you intend to reach."
- Earl Nightingale

"It isn't sufficient just to want—you've got to
ask yourself what are you going to do to
get the things that you want."
- Richard Rose

8. Dorms:
things you'll want to know.

Dorm life! As unique as experiences come, living in the dorms is another one of those "can't miss" college adventures. Scattered pizza boxes, 2:00 a.m. conversations, loud music, dorm food...the college experience is incomplete without experiencing the "dorm phenomena" for at least one year.

Generally, past "dormies" either really loved living in the dorms or they really hated it; very few are neutral. You and your student will have to weigh the pros and cons. Certainly, there are negative aspects to dorm living, but there are a lot of positive things, too. Here's a run through of things to expect:

1. Interesting people, interesting music, interesting times...(atmosphere)
✳ **A priceless cultural experience...**
While living in the dorms, your student will have the opportunity to meet a wide range of interesting, dynamic, and exceptional people. From a star athlete to a genius, from a Congressman's son to a punk rocker, *the dormitories serve as a common home for students from all different backgrounds, experiences, and originating locations.*

✷ A world of differences...

On the other hand, different people have different likes and dislikes. And when you live with people 24 hours-a-day, these differences become extremely evident. Some students might enjoy listening to soft music quietly, while others prefer listening to aggressive music at maximum volume. Different religions...different values...different ideas. *Enjoying dorm living means appreciating others' differences and learning to co-exist with diverse people*...certainly valuable character traits to develop in life.

✷ There is a lot going on, but it is usually not studying...

Dormitories are traditionally not considered the best place to study. Students who have the expectation of getting their studying done in their rooms are probably setting themselves up for failure. It's not impossible, but with students screaming in the halls and loud music echoing from two doors down, it's not recommended.

2. "Hand me a beer!" (partying, etc.)

✷ College students still love to party...

It's impossible to ignore the fact that on many campuses, dormitories are a rather "social" place. Certainly, the fear of law suits has caused colleges and universities to enforce the rules regarding underage drinking much more than they did ten years ago. Still, chances are pretty good that if someone in the dorm is having a party, alcohol will be nearby. Depending on the crowd, marijuana and other drugs might also be present.

For a huge majority of students, college represents the first chance for them to live outside the rules that they had experienced at home. Most students will see this new freedom as a chance to try things that they have never tried or seldom done before.

✳ Explain the consequences...

Do not gloss over lightly the fact that there is a legal drinking age. *The legal consequences of being caught drinking underage are serious, but not nearly as serious as what can happen when young people are drinking and "just having a little fun."* Drinking can lead to more than a head-pounding hangover; it can lead to foolish behavior (such as promiscuity with a stranger) and fatal decisions.

✳ Dorm policies and regulations bring sanity and safety...

Unfortunately, conversations stressing responsibility, making mature decisions, and avoiding potentially harmful situations are going to leave you wishing you could do more. The truth is, you really can't. As hard as you may try, when your student leaves for college he/she's on his/her own.

The good news is that *living in the dorms is one of the safest places* that your student could be during this early transition. Sure, certain influences exist, but, overall, dorm regulations and campus policies have a much better chance of keeping events tame.

3. "What do you mean you live on a co-ed floor?" (co-ed dorms)

✳ Co-ed bathrooms?

One of the great shockers for a lot of parents is the discovery that their son or daughter will be living on a co-ed floor. Although you might be able to get over that little surprise, *understand that at some college campuses co-ed floors might also mean co-ed bathrooms.* Wow!

Even though a certain degree of decorum will be demonstrated by most students, it would not be unusual for your son or daughter to a be brushing his/her teeth in front of the mirror in the evening with someone of the opposite sex...who is only wearing his or her underwear. Other mental pictures could be drawn, but you probably get the idea. In many cases, floor members turn into family members and certain situations are no big deal.

✳ **Another option...**

If the scenario above is one you find worrisome, look into what "co-ed" means at the college your student will be attending. Discuss the situation with your student and see how he/she feels about it. *Same sex floors (and dorms) are always a possibility.*

At many campuses, there are sometimes more students who want to live in the dorms than there are dorm rooms available. If this is true at the college your student will be attending, understand a strong attachment to either one type of living arrangement or another might make it harder to get into the dorms.

4. Hamburgers, dirty socks, and pool tables...(dorm services)

✳ **Three meals a day...**

One feature of the dorms that certainly makes life easier for college students is that they do not have to prepare their own meals. Sure, *it's easy to complain about dorm food, but that's just part of the routine of being in college.* Dorm students save time by not having to worry about grocery shopping and cooking, and parents can be satisfied in knowing that their student is getting three square meals a day.

✶ **Laundry convenience...**

Additionally, now that mom and dad aren't around to do the laundry, students will appreciate the fact that they have easy access to the laundry room. If they can keep straight what colors go with what, they'll only have to worry about finding the motivation to do the laundry. It should also be noted that dollar pinching students always appreciate a donated box of laundry detergent.

✶ **Other amenities...**

Besides appreciating the conveniences of the cafeteria and laundry room, *your student might also enjoy the benefits of having a recreation room and television lounge.* Pool tables, video games, computers, and an assortment of other modes of entertainment will be appreciated during breaks from class and studying. Certainly, dormitory conveniences can make life more comfortable for your student.

5. "Do you live here?" (security and rule enforcement)

✶ **Dorm safeguards...**

A majority of parents, and students, are worried about safety. Of course, it's advisable for your student to be careful no matter where he/she lives, but *living in the dorms is a good choice if security is a major consideration.*

Residents need keys to get into buildings and, at some campuses, door monitors help keep strangers out. *Campus officials make dorm safety a high priority, and it is very likely that security officers will patrol the buildings in the evening.*

✳ Nearby assistance...

If problems arise within the dorm, residential staff members
   are trained to deal with trouble situations and enforce dorm
   rules. If situations turn critical, *staff members are trained
   to know who to contact immediately.* In comparison to
   the security of other living environments, the dorms are
   safe.

If your student is worried about studying late at the library
   and walking back to the dorms, *many campuses have security people to help your student get back to the dorm
   safely.* This should help you relax...somewhat.

6. "You mean two people have to live here?" (the room situation)

✳ Looking at your student's options...

In most dorms, doubles are the prevalent living arrangement
   (two students share a single room). Some dorms also
   have rooms that are triples, and some dorms may even
   have suites (a small group of students share a main living
   area with separate bedrooms). *The literature you receive
   from the college housing office will specifically outline
   your student's options and the costs associated with each.*

✳ Saving money...

*If saving money on housing is of major importance, you may
   want to consider a triple.* The downside, however, is that
   your student will have less privacy having two (or more)
   roommates instead of one. Also, triples aren't that much
   bigger than doubles, so things are very tight and neatness
   becomes a predominant issue. Students living in triples
   are apt to spend more time away from their room than
   students living in doubles, so the positives need to weighed

against the potential negatives.

✳ Sharing a room with a friend can be risky...
If your student plans to room with a friend, make sure that
he/she understands that this sometimes can be a mistake.
Sure it seems like fun to room with a buddy; however, the
level of comfort that exists between the two does not necessarily mean that they will make compatible roommates.
Warn your student of the potential risks.

7. "What's there to do?" (dorm activities)
✳ Regular events throughout the year...
*A terrific benefit of living in the dorms is that there is always
something to do.* Whether it be watching movies in the
lounge, hanging out with friends or going with a group of
people to a campus activity, it's pretty easy to find something to do on a Friday and Saturday night. For students
who have tended to shy away from taking the initiative in
making plans in the past, this is a perfect situation.

✳ The opportunity to be a leader...
If your student is inclined to take the initiative and loves to
plan events, he/she might enjoy participating in the dorm
government or Hall Association. This group of floor rep-
resentatives and elected officers acts as the "social arm"
of the dorm and is responsible for planning activities. It's
a great way for your student to be involved.

Countdown to College

It's a good idea for an in-coming or new student to live in the dorms the first year. Dorm living represents the chance to meet lifetime friends. Sure, the music is loud and the behavior is sometimes unruly, but in the end there is no experience quite like it. Encourage your student to give it a shot.

Words to pass on...

"We shape our buildings; thereafter they shape us."
- Winston Churchill

"We tend to get what we expect."
- Norman Vincent Peale

9. The Greek system:
"rushing" a fraternity or sorority.

Some consider the Greek system one of college's most hallowed pillars. Others categorize it as the source of unbridled chaos and irresponsibility. Whatever your opinion might be, you will be joined by staunch proponents and ardent opponents. Fraternities and sororities represent what many people see as the good in college...and others classify as the not so good.

Referred to as the "Greek system" because of the Greek alphabet used to designate the names of the individual houses, fraternities and sororities have a reputation for promoting wild times. Much of that notoriety isn't entirely undeserved. Here are a few areas that your student should think about before deciding to join the Greek system:

1. "Rushing" a fraternity or sorority...
* What is "rush"?

Fraternity and sorority "rush," usually held the first few weeks of school and sometimes at mid year, *is a process of formal and informal meetings and events sponsored by each individual house within the Greek system.* Members use these events to search for and get an impression of "pledges" (students who are interested in joining the house). During rush, your student will get a general sense of each of the houses by attending events hosted by them. *Membership is by mutual selection.*

✳ Choosing a house...

It's important to remind your son or daughter to thoroughly check out everything about a house during Rush week. Make sure that he/she finds out how much emphasis a house places on academics and what the financial cost to join will be. Just because a house throws great parties doesn't necessarily qualify it as the house to join.

Fraternities and sororities run the gamut. If your son is looking for a house that resembles the Hollywood depiction, he can probably find a suitable match. On the other hand, if your daughter is looking for a more serious house focused on academics or religious beliefs, she can probably find it as well. It is advisable, however, not to be drawn to a house for surface reasons. Remind your teenager not to become caught up in all the hype. *Encourage him/her to examine the legitimate merits of each house.*

✳ Going through "Rush week"...

As Rush week progresses, invitations to return to certain houses will be issued. (Invitations are based on a mutual interest between the house and your son or daughter.) *The key to receiving a "bid" (an invitation to join) is for your son or daughter to make favorable impressions on the members that he or she meets at the Rush functions.* In making a favorable impression, advise your teenager to take the initiative and talk with as many members of the house as possible.

At the individual events, encourage your teenager to *avoid "hanging out" with a friend who is also going through Rush* as this limits the opportunity to meet members who will be making membership decisions. Also, encourage your teenager to not act overly "cool" or pretend to be something that he/she isn't. This behavior will more than likely negate your son or daughter's chances to get into some houses.

* **Dealing with discouragement...**
The whole process of Rush can be very exhilarating. It can also be rather upsetting. If your son or daughter doesn't get into one of his/her top choices, of course there will be a feeling of rejection. Your student will probably feel very hurt, and it's up to you to point out the fact that not everybody we meet in life will like us.

Often, one or two unfavorable impressions can make the difference in not getting into a house. Tell your teenager that the professional world often works the same way, and it's important to take setbacks in stride and move ahead positively. "Sure, disappointment is painful, but don't let it stop you!"

2. The potential benefits in belonging to the Greek system...
Living in a fraternity or sorority does have its benefits, both present and future. Here is a list of potential advantages:

* **Room and board...** Finding a room on some campuses may be benefit enough.
* **Friends...** The opportunity to develop great friends with "brothers and sisters."

✳ **Networking...** Opportunities to network with house alumni could open future doors.

✳ **Social calendar...** An active social calendar that includes beer blasts, silly costume parties and formals can make college a lot of fun.

3. Potential costs in belonging to the Greek system...

The cons of belonging to the Greek system need to be strongly considered. Here is a list of potential disadvantages:

✳ **Expense...** Chapter dues, social dues, and other costs can add up.

✳ **Hazing...** Despite campus policy, hazing continues on some campuses.

✳ **Peer-pressure...** The Greek system is very peer-pressure oriented.

✳ **Elitist...** Sometimes living in a house limits friends to those within the Greek system.

✳ **Time consuming...** Especially for new members, a fraternity or sorority can be very time consuming. House projects, special chores, cleaning up, and the "activities" of pledging can take time away from studying.

The decision to live in a fraternity or sorority is a significant decision and strictly personal. It's important to provide guidance and support to your teenager by discussing with him/her the subject of the Greek system before he/she heads off to school. Waiting until school starts may be too late.

<u>*Words to pass on...*</u>

"*I* *t's been my experience that folks*
who have no vices
have very few virtues."
- Abraham Lincoln

10. Living off campus:
the pros and cons.

In comparison to other alternatives, off-campus living offers the fewest advantages. Certainly, the number of social contacts your student experiences will be reduced drastically. On the other hand, if being completely out on his/her own is your teenager's objective, this is the way to go. Here are a few areas that need to be considered when making the decision of whether or not to agree with your student's off-campus living plans:

1. "This is not quite what I expected."
Doing the grocery shopping, cooking the meals, cleaning the bathroom, dusting...your son or daughter will discover rather quickly that being out on his/her own is not necessarily as glamorous as once thought.

Sure, the freedom might be appealing, but your teenager will probably long for one of mom's terrific home-cooked meals after the first week. Chips and pizza hardly taste as good after having had it seven days in a row.

If you're worried about your teenager's eating habits, look into getting a meal ticket that is good for a couple of meals a day in the dorms. As for cleaning (especially the bathroom), appreciation for one's parents surely begins to grow when faced with the daunting task of cleaning out the toilet bowl.

2. The cost of being on his/her own...
✳ Housing and food.

The chances are good that rent and food costs will not be as high as living in the dorms or in Greek housing. *Even with cheaper food and rent, however, there are additional expenses that can add up* such as cookware, furniture, cleaning supplies, and other miscellaneous items.

Utility bills will come as something of a shock, and it's guaranteed that after a bill or two the heater won't be running 24 hours a day. Money allocated to cover the security deposit and the last month's rent is also known to make a check writer cringe, especially when *the odds of getting the security deposit back are rather slim.* It all begins to add up.

✳ Transportation.

Depending on how far your student lives from campus, transportation becomes an issue. *If your son or daughter takes the car to college, there are certainly additional costs associated with maintaining the car, such as gas, insurance, and perhaps parking.* The bottom line is that you and your son or daughter should sit down with a piece of paper and see how the dollars actually work out for your particular situation..

✳ Time.

The additional hours spent doing tasks that are done for you in the dorm can really accumulate. *Your student will find out that just eating takes a lot of time.* Going to the store, buying groceries, returning home, putting the groceries away, preparing the meal, washing the dishes...this little exercise alone can be a minimum of 7-8 hours a week. After throwing in cleaning, going to the Laundromat, and additional commute time to class, you can see that the extra hours start to be quite significant.

✳ Relationships.
For many students, there is no question that living off campus hinders the opportunity to make friends. *It's just not as easy to develop relationships when you don't have forty floormates with which to hang out.*

✳ Accountability.
If your teenager is going to live out on his/her own, responsibility is critical. By not living in a group setting, your student will not have twenty other students around to hold him/her accountable to study. *Accountability needs to be 100% self-administered.* The example of other students heading off to campus for afternoon classes has pulled more than a few students away from afternoon Soaps, so be careful.

3. Added worries?
✳ Security and safety.
Because of the choice to live off-campus, your teenager will have to deal with certain issues whose importance becomes magnified. *Students who live off-campus are faced with neighborhoods that are more at risk than the well lighted, security patrolled campus facilities.* Additionally, landlords are often a little slower than the college's maintenance staff to fix broken elevators, intercom systems, and security gates.

* Landlord problems.

When looking at an off-campus apartment, it's important to find out how quickly the landlord is in responding to problems. Encourage your student to ask other tenants coming in and out of the building. Your student is definitely going to wish that he/she hadn't overlooked this detail when the heater goes out in December. What he/she is probably going to find is that it's often difficult to get the landlord to get out his checkbook. *Make sure that your student reads the lease thoroughly.*

* Apartment vacancies.

If for some reason or another your teenager's roommate moves out, your son or daughter will be faced with the pressure of filling the vacancy in order to avoid paying double rent. Likewise, your student can literally be left out in the cold if his/her roommate decides to drop out of school the day the rent is due. Make sure that your son or daughter is prepared to deal with this scenario...both mentally and financially.

It is a huge responsibility for your teenager to live on his/her own. If you're picking up the tab for college, it is highly advisable to direct your student to an on-campus environment. Avoid creating unnecessary worry and stress and make sure that the student housing application is filled out completely. And then, cross your fingers and hope that your student gets a spot.

<u>*Words to pass on...*</u>

T he benefits of independent living need to be seriously weighed with the costs of independent living.

"N o alibi will save you from accepting the responsibility."
- Napoleon Hill

11. Commuting:
students who live at home.

Students who live at home and commute to college often feel that they miss out on the college experience. For most commuters, the only thing that they share with other students are the few hours a week where they're actually sitting in class together. Understandably, commuters feel alienated from other students. This is not the best way to enjoy college.

Just because the college that your student will be attending is located in the same city in which you live, there is no a reason for your son or daughter to miss out on the college adventure. With a little prompting from you, and a lot of initiative on the part of your teenager, college can still be a great social and academic experience.

Here are a few tips that can help your student feel more a part of the college community:

1. Ideas to maximize social opportunities for commuting students...

✳ Become involved in campus activities and organizations.

✳ Join a fraternity or sorority.

✳ Join an intramural sports team.

Countdown to College

* Enjoy lunch in the dorms with friends.
* Participate in campus church activities.
* Attend athletic events with other students.
* Get a job on campus.

2. Ideas to maximize <u>learning</u> opportunities for commuting students...

* Become involved in student government.
* Join student study groups.
* Meet with students in your class.
* Study in the campus library.
* Utilize the resources of the campus learning center.
* Become involved with the school paper.
* Return to campus to attend special lectures and events in the evenings and on weekends.

If your son or daughter will be commuting, strongly encourage him/her to take the initiative in meeting people and becoming involved. Students who live on campus naturally feel a part of the college scene. *Your student will have to work harder in order to feel a part of things.*

Instead of your student being disappointed by not receiving invitations to go out or be involved, *encourage him/her to take an active role in planning his/her social calendar.* Sure, it probably means more time in the car going back and forth from campus, but that is the cost of maximizing the college experience.

<u>*Words to pass on...*</u>

*C**ommuting is exactly what you make of it. Good or bad.*

*"N**othing happens by itself. . . . It all will come your way, once you understand that you have to make it come your way, by your own exertions."*
- Ben Stein

12. Dating:
areas of concern...yours and theirs.

Meeting fun people and developing new relationships is one of the perks that comes with "the job" for a college student. Certainly, very few of us have the opportunity to meet as many people over the course of a year as we did in college. The chance to meet new people is everywhere - in the dorms, in class, at games, at parties, etc. For many, college friends become lifetime friends.

Undoubtedly, you probably worry about the kinds of friends your son or daughter will meet. Most parents do. Recording even higher on the "parent worry scale," however, is whom your kid will date. Will your all-American son bring home a Madonna look-alike? Will your conservative daughter be attracted to a motorcycle riding, leather-jacket-wearing guy with spiked, purple hair? A parent's imagination has no bounds.

Parents usually have concerns much different from their students regarding the subject of college dating. Here's a look at both:

1. Parents concerns...

Knowing that your son or daughter is away at college on a
 first date with someone whom you've never met is probably not a thought that gives you warm fuzzies. It is a
 thought that probably makes you rather nervous, though.
 Here are a few suggestions that you should make sure to
 pass on to your student:

✶ Encourage group dates.

*Going out with a group of friends, rather than a formal date,
 is a safe way to get to know someone better.* If your teenager doesn't want to date in groups, strongly convey the
 importance of having him/her tell roommates who he/she
 will be with (including phone number), where he/she is
 going, and what time he/she will be back.

✶ Encourage good judgment.

*Stress the importance of going home or contacting a friend
 immediately if your student starts to get a bad feeling about
 someone while on a date.* This certainly includes not getting into the car with a date who has been drinking. (A
 very valuable going away gift is a cellular phone that can
 be used in emergency situations.)

✶ Encourage being safe.

If your student is sexually active, stress with every ounce of
 energy the absolute 100% necessity to be safe in order to
 avoid pregnancy and disease.

2. Students' concerns...

✶ "I don't have any money!" (dating on a limited bud-get)

Poverty is a continuous condition for most college students, so the appeal for "dating money" is common. Instead of being swayed by even the greatest of emotional pleas, remind your student of all the terrific and inexpensive dates that are possible.

(1) campus movies or video rental

(2) campus recitals

(3) campus sporting events

(4) board games & popcorn

(5) tennis

(6) picnic on campus

(7) going to parties together

(8) studying together

(9) going to a coffee shop

(10) pool or video games

...the list is long and only limited by the thought that a lot of money needs to be spent in order to have fun. And, by the way, *it is acceptable to share the cost of dates.* Just work it out beforehand.

✴ **"I never meet anybody!" (meeting people)**
Although this alleviates a few of your worries, it might cause your teenager a bit of anguish. With your student's interest in mind, advise *him/her that meeting people often means taking the initiative.* Offering the following suggestions might lead to new friends and relationships:

(1) Take the first step...
Encourage your student to borrow class notes from someone.

Suggest repaying the courtesy by treating the individual providing the notes to a cup of coffee. Or, with the endless lines that a college student has to stand in, propose striking up conversations with others who are also waiting in line.

(2) Change hangouts...

Suggest hanging out on a different dorm floor/lounge, a different library, or a different part of campus. *New scenery will bring new people.*

(3) Get active...

Recommend that your student become active in a campus club. The more involved your student is, the greater the opportunity he/she will have to meet new people.

Through all the trials and tribulations that come with dating, an occasional *"Now don't forget to study!"* reminder is probably necessary. Remind your student to stay focused on school and keep it as the #1 priority.

<u>*Words to pass on...*</u>

B oyfriends and girlfriends come and go, but transcripts are forever.

13. Religion:
finding fellowship on campus.

Despite what you might fear, *churches abound and flourish on college campuses* across the country. Whether it be worship services, Bible studies, seminars, or retreats, your son or daughter will have ample opportunity to be involved in a group or church that meets your approval. Although your son or daughter might miss the church that he/she has grown up with, it is highly likely that your student will be able to find a new and comfortable church that he/she can call "home."

1. Finding the right church.
If you are fearful that your son or daughter might not find the right church, or if finding a quality church for your student is a top priority, you can always *ask your home church leader to help you in the search process.*

Perhaps the leader might be familiar with a strong church already, and if not, he/she certainly has the ability to get that information. If a certain denomination is strongly desired, this is one way to make sure that you're sending your freshman in the right direction. *Knowing that your student will be attending a church recommended by some-*

one you know can be very comforting.

2. College ministries...

Often, churches near colleges have very well developed and
dynamic college ministries dedicated to catering to the
needs of the student. Some churches even have a special
service just for college students.

Additionally, *college ministries do an excellent job of creat-*
ing a social environment in which students enjoy partici-
pating. Whether it be throwing theme parties, fielding
intramural teams, participating in community activities,
or just coordinating a once-a-week dinner, college ministries are extremely active.

3. Religious organizations on campus...

Besides the church, *your son or daughter can find spiritual*
support by joining campus religious organizations, such
as Campus Crusade. *Some theme houses within the Greek*
system are also committed to following certain religions.
Whatever religion, your student should be able to find
what he/she is seeking.

4. A special warning regarding cults...

Known to frequent college campuses, cults often prey on students who have been shaken by the realities of life. In a
time of searching, some students find the open and accepting arms of the cult to be very appealing. *It is prob-*
ably a wise decision to investigate unfamiliar groups in
which your student becomes involved.

Considering the pressure some students inevitably feel regarding school, it's a good idea to encourage your student to

be involved in a local church or religious organization. *Having the opportunity to be a part of the supportive atmosphere that a church can provide can be a tremendous lift to a struggling student.*

<u>*Words to pass on...*</u>

*"**G**ood, the more communicated,*
more abundant grows."
- John Milton

A time to learn...academics.

14. Recommended classes:
classes that can make a difference.

Some courses simply make a semester more enjoyable. Other courses can help develop and sharpen skills that will be instrumental in shaping your son or daughter's future. Here are a few courses that you should encourage your student to consider taking:

1. Critical thinking courses.
Philosophy and rhetoric are excellent courses to take in training the mind to think. Exacting exercises and assignments help develop an ability to constructively analyze issues and ideas.

2. Courses that familiarize students with campus resources.
Mentioned earlier, *courses that establish familiarity with the campus library and research system can be extraordinarily useful* in helping your student succeed in college. Sometimes called Bibliography, this particular course challenges

the student to become fully acquainted with the tools necessary to write expanded research projects and future term papers.

3. Communication courses.

Interpersonal communication courses, usually found in the education department, can be invaluable for enhancing listening and communication skills.

4. Writing courses.

Although the suggestion of taking a writing course might be met with waning enthusiasm, the lifetime benefits of being able to communicate on paper are immeasurable. *The ability to write well is a talent that can be developed.*

5. Current issue courses.

Often, guest lecturers address issues pertaining to state, national and world concerns. The perspectives offered are from newsmakers who are intimately involved with the issues. *These courses are frequently found in the political science department.*

6. Fun courses!

Learning doesn't always have to be a mental grind! You'll be a real hero if you mention that your son or daughter should consider taking a course such as art appreciation, sailing, or golf. These courses can provide a needed break in the schedule; plus, they have lifetime benefits.

<u>Words to pass on...</u>

*"**T**he time to repair the roof is
when the sun is shining."*
- John F. Kennedy

*"**L**et our advance worrying
become advance thinking and planning."*
- Winston Churchill

*"**I**f I went back to college again, I'd
concentrate on two areas: learning to write
and speak before an audience."*
- President Gerald R. Ford

15. Class schedules:
helping choose a first semester schedule.

The first semester of college is your student's most important term. Put yourself in your son or daughter's shoes. Perhaps you're leaving home for the first time. You're leaving your friends, the comfort of high school, and even the security of the family pet. These changes are more than likely going to be very dramatic.

Sure, your young prodigy might seem to be brimming with confidence, but undoubtedly that confidence is masking more than a little uncertainty. It is extremely important, therefore, to build on the confidence and not the uncertainty by helping your student achieve early success in the first semester.

Taking the time to help select a class schedule becomes one of the most important things you can do in assuring success for your student the first year. Here are a few hints to guide you and your student in selecting a first semester schedule geared towards success:

1. Ease in lightly.
There is nothing to prove by taking a heavy unit load (16+ units). *A well-balanced schedule between the 12-15 unit*

mark will allow your son or daughter the opportunity to achieve confidence in building grades. There will be plenty of time to make up units over the next four years. The important thing is to allow him or her to be acclimated without being overwhelmed.

2. Introductory courses are not necessarily the easiest.

Don't think that a course is easy because it has a 1, 2, or 3 after it (i.e., Chemistry 1, Political Science 3). *Some introductory courses are extremely difficult and time consuming.* Many students find some introductory courses so difficult that they make the decision to avoid that particular area of study ever again! (Additionally, future courses in that same subject area might be much more interesting, so make sure that your son or daughter doesn't avoid them!)

Also, it's not uncommon for many students to have to take a remedial English course their first year. Even if your son or daughter was an "A" student in high school English, he/she might still find him/herself doing less than satisfactory in early papers. *However, do not think for a moment that "bonehead" English is a breeze or that your son or daughter shouldn't be there.*

This course can be graded particularly tough in order to prepare students for the writing standards of the college. Make sure to keep your own ego in check and appreciate the fact that your student is going to have the opportunity to receive some strong writing fundamentals.

3. Seek out the course that makes other college courses easier.

Many colleges offer a course that builds familiarity with the campus library and research system. Often called Library Science, Introduction To College, or Bibliography 1, this course challenges the student to become acquainted with the tools necessary to write expanded research projects and future term papers. These courses could prove to be the most important courses your son or daughter ever takes.

4. 8:00 a.m.: success or disaster.

In a perfect world, 8:00 a.m. classes are not a big deal. The problem is, however, late night discussions and pizza parties end up taking a toll. Some students miss class by telling themselves that they can sleep in if they get notes from a classmate. This scenario is the recipe for academic disaster! *Attending class is crucial, so encourage classes that start no earlier than 9:00 a.m.* This comfort zone can make a difference.

Likewise, attending classes at the end of the day is not a good idea either. It's tough to consistently turn down the desire to join floormates out on the intramural field. Most students are academically inclined between the hours of 9:00 a.m.-3:00 p.m.; in order to avoid temptation, it's smart for your student to build a schedule accordingly.

5. Bunching brings problems.

A good schedule is spread out across the week. Although many students like to bunch classes on a Monday/Wednesday or on a Tuesday/Thursday, it is not the best idea. By attending all of his/her classes in just two days, your student can get "lecture overload." *Retention and attention have the tendency to be higher when you don't have to attend one lecture after another.*

Also, a day with no classes often turns into a day with no studying. Some students might like to believe that by having all their classes on Tuesday/Thursday they would be able to study all day on Monday, Wednesday, and Friday. It is, however, a rare occasion when the M/W/F agenda is followed.

6. Switch gears.

It is a good idea to break up a 100% science schedule with a liberal arts class and vice versa. Many students find the slight change of focus to be refreshing and stimulating. It will also help your student receive a more complete education.

7. It's O.K. to schedule a fun course.

Encourage your student to take a fun class! How about archery or sailing? Perhaps a drama class for those so inclined. Whatever the class might be, *having fun in the classroom can help your student maintain a positive attitude in his/her other courses.*

<u>*Words to pass on...*</u>

"Success occurs when
opportunity meets preparation."
- John Wooden

Proceeding with caution
is rarely a bad idea.

16. Studying:
helping establish good study habits.

Establishing effective study habits is crucial if your son or daughter is to realize academic success. Unfortunately, monitoring performance in this particular area is impossible. Often, your only indication of whether or not effective studying is taking place is when grades are released.

With so many exciting "distractions" flaunting their appeal, it's easy to see why studying sometimes takes a back seat to extra-curricular events. You remember...dating, basketball games, hanging out with the people on the floor, fraternity parties. *The key is for your student to incorporate these activities into his/her schedule without neglecting his/her studies.*

Here are a few valuable tips that you should make sure to pass on to your college student. Time spent sharing these tips now will pay big dividends for your student later.

1. Write it down!
The value of keeping a master schedule of the semester can not be overstated! *Besides keeping a day-to-day organizer, you should insist that your student keep a master desk calendar that includes every assignment and test that*

is do. This terrific reminder system makes it impossible for due dates to sneak up on anyone.

2. Stress time management.

Students who achieve high grades successfully manage their time. *Just as classes and dorm meals are scheduled at specific times during the day, specific times should also be set aside for studying.*

Look at blocks of time (i.e., 2:00 p.m. - 5:00 p.m.) that are available after lectures, labs, and sections have been accounted for in the daily schedule, and encourage your student to fill in open blocks with "mandatory" study time. *Only by building accountability into his/her schedule is your student going to assure having adequate study and preparation time.*

3. Location, location, location.

Finding a regular location to study is a smart idea. Studying in the same location is a signal to work. Encourage your student to check out campus libraries in order to find a satisfactory location and, thus, minimalize potential distractions. Convince your student that no matter what, his/her room is not a satisfactory location to study. The temptation to watch TV, talk on the phone, and even fall asleep are just too great.

4. Concentration problems.

If your son or daughter complains of an inability to concentrate, there are a few suggestions that you can provide:

Countdown to College

✴ **Alternate subjects periodically.**

Changing subject matter (even for 15 minutes) is often just the break the brain was needing. It is then possible to go back to the original subject more energized.

✴ **Listen to up-tempo music during breaks.**

This is especially helpful if sleepiness is an issue. Encourage your student to take a walkman to the library and listen to it during short study breaks.

✴ **Exercise.**

If sleepiness is a problem, encourage your student to develop a regular exercise schedule. Exercise can make a big difference in breaking concentration problems.

✴ **Be an active reader.**

After he/she reads a short passage, suggest that your student summarize to him/herself what he/she's just read. This practice will keep your student sharp and alert. It also prevents the need to go back and read a section over just because he/she can't remember what it was that he/she just read.

A good goal for your son or daughter to establish is to study in blocks of 50 minutes and then take a 10 minute break to get fresh air and stretch. Practicing the above principles should make that goal very reasonable.

Words to pass on...

The benefits of working hard far outweigh the price of hard work.

"Quality is not an act. It is a habit."
- Aristotle

Perseverance is the hard work you do after you get tired of doing the hard work you already did.

17. First exams:

helping deal with a poor grade on an early exam or paper.

Certainly, nothing has the potential to deflate the college experience faster for your son or daughter than receiving a bad grade. The early successes that he/she found (i.e., new friends and fitting in) will be forgotten and "college" will once again take the form of something dark and menacing.

Feeling as if the rug has been pulled out from underneath his/her feet, your student's self-confidence might show itself for what it probably has been all along...shaky. If your student had always received superior grades in high school, he/she will more than likely be shocked at this change of fortune.

It's important to be prepared to step in at this time and add a little bit of rational thinking to an emotional situation. Here are four areas that can help push your son or daughter past this early obstacle:

1. Feedback from you. ("Great! Now, you know what to avoid next time!")
Don't support negative thinking! Nothing can be more valuable at this time than for you to remain positive and up-

beat. Take the news in stride and make sure that your son or daughter understands that a bad grade isn't "the end of the world." Help negate the negative thoughts spinning through your student's mind by putting a positive spin on the situation. A bad grade isn't anything that should cause panic.

2. Feedback the test taker gives himself. ("I'll look at my exam again...")

After giving needed reinforcement, ask your son or daughter to step away from the emotions of the situation and honestly assess his/her work as if he/she was looking at the work of a complete stranger. Encourage your student to study his/her mistakes.

Have your student ask: *"Did I follow the assignment? Did I really spend adequate time studying? Did I understand the material?"* He/she might find this honest evaluation of his/her own work to be particularly interesting and informative.

3. Feedback from the test grader. ("What I look for in papers is this...")

Objective self-evaluation can certainly help your son or daughter determine why he/she got that particular grade. Still, *it's advisable to meet individually with the person responsible for giving the grade.* (Was it the teaching assistant or the professor?)

By seeking feedback, your son or daughter not only has the chance to receive constructive criticism regarding this assignment, but also insight into what the grader specifically looks for in determining "A" and "B" grades. Knowing what the grader is looking for can lead to a further understanding now and greater confidence later.

4. Feedback from campus services. ("There's a course on test strategy...")

This is a terrific time for your son or daughter to check out the available academic counseling services on campus. *Special courses on overcoming test anxiety, preparing for tests, and understanding test strategies are among a few courses that the campus probably offers.* These services aren't exclusively for students doing poorly...just students who want to get good grades.

Words to pass on...

*T*hose who don't take the time to learn from failures shouldn't be surprised when they repeat them.

18. Mid-terms & finals:
helping deal with the pressure.

Very few are immune to experiencing the panic of final exams. No student looks forward to that dreaded week or to the preceding weeks that are dedicated to studying and preparing for the exams. Likewise, very few college experiences are as glorious as the one when a student strolls out of his/her last final. The feeling of "tremendous relief" at that moment is universal with students everywhere.

As a parent of one going through the "finals indoctrination," be prepared to relive your own magical moments of final exams past. After grimacing at your own memories of last hour cramming, remember that your son or daughter might find it valuable if you were to pass on some pain easing information.

"Finals Blues" can't be averted altogether, but there is a remedy that minimalizes its nerve-racking effect. That remedy is P-R-E-P-A-R-A-T-I-O-N. *Success in getting through this stressful period is a result of being academically and emotionally ready to perform.*

1. Academic preparation...
Nothing is better at alleviating the stress of finals than "know-

ing your stuff." Familiarity with the subject material breeds a confidence that makes the stress of finals manageable. In the case that your son or daughter is suffering a confidence problem because of a <u>lack</u> of subject familiarity, it's time to get familiar. Here are a few tips that will help your student get up to speed:

✳ **Attend <u>every</u> pre-exam study session.**

These sessions, hosted by the professor or teaching assistant, will be dedicated to going over information that will be on the test. *They are invaluable in helping your son or daughter determine what he/she should study* the last few days before the exam.

✳ **Review tests of past exams.**

Suggest that your student review copies of past exams. A campus library will probably have a file of the old exams.

✳ **Encourage a meeting with the grader.**

By knowing a few things about what the grader might be looking for, your student *will gain insight into test strategy and, perhaps, test content.* Asking for direction never hurts. Who knows what valuable "bone" the grader might throw out.

2. Emotional preparation...

Equally important, *emotional preparation means doing things that add to a positive mental state.* It means taking care of your physical and mental condition. Failure by your son or daughter to do this can result in multiplying the effects of stress. Here are some suggestions that you should share:

✶ Exercise.

If your son or daughter has never been an exerciser, now is the time to start. *A vigorous aerobic workout will do wonders for the nerves.* There is no better stress reducer than exercise.

✶ Don't neglect sleep.

Final exams is often a time when sleep is neglected. When this happens, stress has the chance to affect the body even harder. Remind your son or daughter that not only will he/she feel much better, but his/her mind will be much sharper if he/she keeps a consistent sleep pattern during final exams.

✶ Look into stress reduction courses.

Remind your son or daughter to look into the special courses the campus offers in regard to stress reduction. These classes have proven to be a valuable resource in helping students deal with the pressure that comes with finals.

✶ Avoid alcohol and junk food!

A poor diet can add to the problem and increase the impact stress has on the body. Send a healthy Care Package.

✶ For temporary relief of stress, focus on breathing.

Have your student practice taking full, deep breaths while counting to five. *Hold each breath for the count of twenty (4 times longer than the inhale), and then slowly release the breath while counting to ten.* Repeating this formula five times in a row and three times a day will help reduce stress. (Formula: inhale 1x, hold 4x, exhale 2x).

<u>*Words to pass on...*</u>

"*T*here is no victory at bargain basement prices."
- *Dwight David Eisenhower*

"*S*ingleness of purpose is one of the chief essentials for success in life, no matter what may be one's aim."
- *John D. Rockefeller, Jr.*

19. Academic overload:
helping get through a tough semester.

Some semesters are just nightmares. At least, that's certainly how they seem at the time. As soon as your student finishes the ten page paper that he/she's been working on most of the semester, he/she can look forward to cramming for the three upcoming mid-term exams. The part that your freshman is really dreading, however, is the 25 page term paper that counts for 85% of the grade in his/her political science class.

Whether it be attempting a hero's schedule of 18+ units, or just trying to find a way to get through the semester where everything has gone wrong, tough semesters have not gotten any easier. Nothing is more anticipated than hearing the sound of the bell at 2:00 p.m. on Thursday, June 3...the time the last final of the semester has come to an end.

There is little you can do to make a tough semester easier for your student. *What you can do, though, is make it a lot more bearable.* After you're through doing the "parent thing" (i.e., "Take it a day at a time...make sure you get enough sleep...eat right...exercise to reduce the stress"), you can do a few things that will probably be a bit more appreciated.

Countdown to College
1. Do something special!

Plan a surprise for your student that will be sure to leave him/ her smiling at the memory for days. *Do something that breaks the monotony of studying day-after-day.* Let your son or daughter know that you love him/her. Here are a few ideas:

* Send a care package that includes a special gift.
* Visit him/her on campus for a few hours.
* Send a cheerful flower or balloon bouquet.
* Send him/her money to take a friend out to dinner.
* Send a fun video or audio tape that the family has made.
* Contact a favorite celebrity and see if the person will send your student an autographed photo.

2. Be a fan!

Sending weekly notes of encouragement can really provide a needed lift. The notes don't have to be lengthy, just extremely supportive. Tell your student that you're very proud of him/her! Be positive and encourage your freshman to finish strong!

<u>*Words to pass on...*</u>

*"**N**ever give up then, for that is just the place and time that the tide will turn."*
- Harriet Beecher Stow

*"**P**rocrastination is opportunity's natural assassin."*
- Victor Kiam

20. Hard classes:
helping get through difficult courses.

There is only <u>one</u> thing that can help your son or daughter get through a difficult course successfully...*hard work!* No magic secrets here. Just plain, old-fashioned, roll-up-the-sleeves tenacity. It's your job to relay that information.

Unfortunately, many students tend to ignore this principle and <u>avoid</u> hitting the books harder for a tough class. *Human nature causes us to shy away from things that are stressful and uncomfortable.* Tough classes are the classes where studying is put off for the sake of doing something else. Anything else!

As a parent, your job is to assist in transforming the mindset of your student from one of trepidation and anxiety to eagerness and hunger. The "tough class" scenario represents your best opportunity to play the roll of coach and motivator. *"Forget the grade! Take this class head on! Learn and understand the material so well that you could teach it!"*

A change in mindset should bring a change in your student's study plan as well. Latin or chemistry will no longer be a course that your student dreads picking up the book for, but rather hungrily waits to attack! Here are four suggestions to share:

1. Don't be intimidated!

Suggest to your student that he/she enter every class with a feeling of anticipation of what might be learned, not intimidation of what isn't known.

2. Participate!

Recommend that your student be aggressive and participate in sections and labs.

3. Attend office hours!

Encourage your son or daughter to visit the professor and teaching assistant during office hours for further discussion of lectures and course texts.

4. Seek out every opportunity to learn!

Challenge your student to seek out every study group possible, including checking the campus learning center for additional opportunities.

A change of attitude and an aggressive approach can make all the difference. Have your student ignore the fact that tough classes are demanding, and accept the challenge that these classes are "mountains to be climbed!" The key is to go for it!

Words to pass on...

*"**N**o man is ever whipped, until he quits . . .*
in his own mind."
- Napoleon Hill

*"**P**lodding wins the race."*
- Aesop

*"**T**ry, try, try and keep trying is the rule*
that must be followed to become
an expert in anything."
- W. Clement Stone

21. Bad semesters:
helping to avoid a repeat performance.

Let's assume that your son or daughter didn't heed 100% of your wisdom in getting through Physics 10 (the last section: **Hard classes:** *helping get through difficult courses*). In fact, not only did your student manage to receive a bad grade in physics, but his/her grades in Statistics 21 and History 17B easily bring a grimace to your face.

Receiving one bad grade doesn't necessarily characterize a semester as bad. Strong or satisfactory grades in other classes can definitely help balance out a GPA. *Two bad grades, though, represent an unquestionable lock on the label "bad semester" and can drive a GPA into the ground.*

Obviously, this is the time to help your student regroup. Something didn't go right. The question is "What?" Strongly encourage your student to take the time to objectively analyze his/her mistakes. *By asking questions related to material comprehension, study habits, and time management, you help your student learn from his/her mistakes.*

Here are a few solutions that could solve the specific problem that your student may have:

1. If your student is having trouble understanding the material...

✳ He/she should attend <u>every</u> discussion section and lecture.

✳ He/she should visit the professor and/or teaching assistant during office hours.

✳ He/she should look into getting a tutor.

✳ He/she should find a study partner who is an "A" student.

2. If your student is having difficulty finding the time to prepare...

✳ He/she should prioritize his/her schedule so that school comes first.

✳ He/she should mark a calendar with test and due dates and plan preparation time accordingly.

3. If your student is doing poorly on writing assignments or labs...

✳ He/she should seek out specific feedback from the grader.

✳ He/she should take a writing course in order to help develop technique and style.

✳ He/she should sit in on labs and sections other than his/her own.

✳ When papers are returned, he/she should examine the "A" papers of other students.

4. If your student is having difficulty keeping up with the work load...

✳ He/she should consider taking a reduced unit load.

✳ He/she should prioritize work more effectively.

✳ He/she should start semester writing assignments and major projects immediately.

5. If your student is having a tough time concentrating...

✳ He/she should begin an exercise program.

✳ He/she should learn stress reduction techniques.

✳ He/she should monitor sleep and eating habits.

6. If your student is getting nervous during tests...

✳ He/she should learn relaxation techniques.

✳ He/she should spend adequate time preparing for exams and avoid cramming.

✳ He/she should discuss the situation with the professor or teaching assistant.

7. If your student is having difficulty getting along with instructors...

✳ He/she should remember who gives the grades!

At this point, your student has two choices. *He/she can either look at his/her grades and be miserable, or he/she can evaluate the reasons why his/her grades were bad and make sure to avoid the same mistakes in the future.* Help your student choose the latter.

<u>*Words to pass on...*</u>

"Always bear in mind that your own resolution to succeed is more important than any other one thing."
- Abraham Lincoln

Remember, failure is an event—not a person. Encourage your student to learn from a bad semester.

22. Studying abroad:
weighing the benefits versus the costs.

Although usually reserved for students who have a year or two of college under their belt, *studying abroad can be a fantastic, unforgettable, and maturing experience.* Whether it be for the entire year or just the summer, you might find the idea of your son or daughter studying overseas to be appealing. If you're neutral on the subject, however, be prepared to have the topic mentioned by an eager student at some time in the future.

The reason for giving thought now to the possibility of your student studying abroad is strictly financial. For some families, the cost of a program might be inconsequential in their decision. For others, it might be monumental. *If money will be the deciding issue in whether or not your student goes abroad, now is the time to start planning...and saving.*

1. Considerations <u>before</u> deciding whether or not to go abroad...

✶ **The benefits of participating:**

(1) The opportunity to travel.

(2) The experience of living in another country.

(3) Learning a foreign language in the host country.

(4) Enhancing the total educational experience.

(5) Increased knowledge in a specific area (music, architecture, art, etc.)

In deciding whether or not to study abroad, ask yourself, *"What is our objective?"* Quite possibly, other options might meet your objectives just as well, such as taking a family trip or traveling with a volunteer organization or church group for the summer.

✱ **The costs of participating...**

(1) Money.

(2) Student might not get anything out of the experience.

(3) Distance from family.

(4) Possibility that other opportunities might suffer because of the decision to go (i.e., internships, athletic practices, etc.).

You and your student have to make the determination of whether or not the benefits outweigh the costs in regard to your family's individual situation. *Ask questions and seek input from students and families who have previously participated.*

2. Considerations after making the decision to go abroad:

✱ **Does the objective of the program match our objective?**

Some programs might emphasize travel and sightseeing, while others are more focused on academics. If your student is looking for a program with a more specific theme such as music, art, or learning a foreign language, it more than likely exists. *Campus resources should help your student find exactly the program that he/she is seeking.*

✳ What do program costs include?

Will there be additional charges for sightseeing and transportation? How much will food and housing cost? What insurance is provided as part of the program cost? How much is additional insurance coverage? Are there added costs for books and supplies?

✳ What will the housing situation be like?

What is the quality and age of the accommodations? In what part of town are they located? Is there adequate security? What does a sample menu look like?

✳ Who will be doing the teaching?

What are the credentials of the instructional staff? Are they full-time or part-time?

✳ What will the academic schedule be like?

How much time will there be for touring? Are there planned trips through the program or will the students be on their own? Is it possible to get a specific week-by-week schedule? What background learning should the student have before arriving?

✳ What is the background of the other students?

Where are the other students from? What year in school are they? What students from your son or daughter's college will be participating in the program?

✳ What is the refund policy if my son or daughter has to leave early?

For whatever reason the program isn't completed, what is the refund policy?

✶ How are the medical services?

What quality of medical care will be available during the duration of the program? What is the quality of the emergency care? How will insurance coverage work? Who in the program can I talk with if something happens?

Additional tips:

Encourage your student to familiarize himself with the culture and language of the country in which he/she will be studying. Before leaving, encourage your student to contact other students who will be participating in the program.

Words to pass on...

"*P*lanning is bringing the future into the present so that you can do something about it now."
- Alan Lakein

23. Summer school:
is it for your student?

If your student needs to take an extra course, summer school is a terrific option. *Although there are many good reasons for your student to hit the books for the summer, there are a few reasons that he/she should avoid taking classes as well.* Evaluate the list below with your student and decide which course of action would be more beneficial.

Reasons to say "Yes to summer school"...
1. Fill in educational gaps.
Summer school is a great time to encourage your student to take that math or writing course that he/she hasn't yet taken. Maybe a college level American history or geography course would be helpful. With your student, *determine what subjects might help balance his/her education and fill in the educational gaps.*

2. Chance to take fun courses.
It's sometimes difficult to fit in a specific course during the year. If there is a course that your student thinks will be fun to take, summer school is the time.

3. Repeat courses.
If your student has had to take an "incomplete," summer

school is a the perfect time to finish the course (especially if he/she had struggled with the course previously).

4. Graduate early or on time.

Many students find it difficult to graduate in four years. Because of a demanding study load or some other activity, your student might be behind on the four year goal. In order to get back on track, he/she might consider summer school.

5. Preparation for future courses.

If a tough course looms in the future and your student doesn't feel prepared to handle it, he/she should *consider taking background courses.* This will help ease future anxiety and allow your student the opportunity to succeed in that future course.

6. Opportunity to build GPA.

Summer school could be a chance for your student to build his/her GPA. Taking an elective or two during the summer could help balance the Chemistry 1A grade.

7. Save money.

Attending summer school often means cheaper tuition. If maximizing tuition dollars is important, summer school is recommended.

8. Experience a different school or part of the country for the summer.

Perhaps your student has an interest in attending an Ivy League or other top notch school for the summer. Maybe spending the summer on the east coast is particularly appealing. Summer school represents the chance to do both of these things.

Reasons to say "No" to summer school...
1. Miss opportunity to make money with full-time summer job.
If your student needs to work at a full-time job during the summer to help pay for school for the rest of the year, summer school is not for him/her.

2. Work experience opportunities are sacrificed.
By attending summer school, your student sacrifices the chance to gain work experience. The cost of passing up an internship and career networking opportunities needs to be carefully weighed against the benefits of taking summer courses.

3. Burnout from going to school continuously.
Students who make the decision to attend summer school need to be careful that they don't get academic burnout. Some students will find it very challenging to stay motivated throughout the summer and then into the fall without a break. *Fall grades have the potential of suffering if your student experiences burnout.*

A special note on students attending summer school at another campus...
Advise your student to check with the Admissions office to make sure that the classes that he/she wants to take at another campus are transferable for full credit to his/her home college. If the units are not fully transferable, the two of you will need to decide if the summer program is worth attending. Likewise, *make sure that your student fills out the nec-*

essary paperwork to have the summer units transferred back
to the home college.

<u>*Words to pass on...*</u>

*B efore making the decision to
go to summer school, ask first...
"What is my #1 objective?"*

A time to prepare...
situations of conflict

24. Fear:
helping overcome college intimidation.

It's seems odd that something that was looked forward to with such excitement is now looked upon with fear, insecurity, and even dread when the actual moment comes. As the time to leave draws closer, reality starts to set in for your college bound teenager. Confidence begins to erode as an internal voice starts booming loudly inside your teenager's head:

> *"Hey, you better start getting nervous because you're heading off to college next month! What are you going to do now that you really have to start studying? Do you think that you'll even understand the material? You're in big trouble now!"*

Sure, the thought of going to college is exciting, but it can also be very intimidating. As the summer before the freshman year comes to a close, self-doubt slowly begins to creep in and major worries start to build. Consider bringing these worries out into the open by sensitively discussing them with your son or daughter.

1. Worry: "How am I going to keep up with the studying?"

By now, your teenager has probably hit the panic button after hearing a few horror stories concerning the amount of studying college students have to do. Before the panic level gets too extreme, remind your freshman that a heavy study workload can be overcome with a commitment to two simple words...time management.

* Time management is crucial!

It's no secret that keeping up with one's studies means allocating the necessary time to get the job done. If a total of 30 hours is needed to complete a specific project, then those 30 hours need to be worked into a time schedule. Whether it be organizing the hours of a day, the days of a week, or the weeks in a semester, your teenager needs to learn how to master his/her time.

Because most college bound students are weak in this area, your student will probably find that he/she needs to polish his/her skills in order to deal with the quantity of work that professors assign. *There is no substitute in regard to putting in the time.*

2. Worry: "Am I going to be able 'to cut it' academically?"

Some students might be leery of their own ability to succeed at the next academic level ("What if I don't understand a thing that the professor is talking about?"). If this is a worry for your student, take the time to discover in which subject area(s) your freshman is concerned.

✳ Writing well is a must!

For most majors, being a good writer is crucial. In fact, a grade can often hinge on how well a student can analyze a position or idea, and then either defend or criticize that point of view. Whether it be an exam, a term project, or just a weekly writing assignment, the ability to communicate on paper is the #1 grade determinant.

✳ Brush up in summer school.

Some students find it helpful to take a summer writing course at their local community college before starting school in the fall. Depending on your student's needs, other summer courses that can sharpen skills, such as math and time management, can also be beneficial.

3. Worry: "What if the other students are smarter than me?"

It can be very intimidating for your son or daughter to start comparing him/herself with other students. Sure, there will be some freshman who are smarter; there will probably be 4.0 superstars everywhere. There will also be students who have traveled throughout the world and others who have gone to the finest prep schools. The fact is, there will also be students who have had far fewer advantages.

✳ Doing your best is what matters most.

Impress upon your teenager to not worry about who is sitting next to him/her, but to worry only about doing his/her own personal best. *Using one's own yardstick of achievement is far better than measuring oneself up against someone else's.*

4. Worry: "What am I going to do without my friends?"

The realization that trusted friends and family won't be nearby can be very upsetting. Undoubtedly, this can add to household tensions and dramatic mood swings as your teenager begins to understand the consequences of leaving home (especially for the first time). To your teenager, *this "rite of passage" might mean heading to an unknown environment without the support of people who have always been there.*

✱ Friends and family are only a phone call away.

Let your student know that just because friends and family won't physically be close, they can still be a significant part of his/her life. *Letters, phone calls, campus visits...all of these things will allow your student to share his/her college experience with those who are closest to him/her.* Great relationships don't have to disappear with distance.

5. Worry: "Will I meet new friends?"

Although few teenagers will admit it to their parents, the majority of college bound freshman are somewhat nervous about fitting in to their new environment. "Will I make new friends? Will the fraternity or sorority accept me? Will my roommate like me?" While putting up a confident front, your teenager is probably feeling a little insecure about the ability to develop future friendships.

✱ Uncertainty is normal.

Regardless of how solid your student's goals and plans are, freshman are going to be nervous about whether or not others will like them. In the days and weeks prior to leaving, it is natural for the universal fear of "being rejected" to begin to hit peak levels. Share with your teenager that it is normal to have these feelings. In fact, *the vast majority of freshman are probably experiencing these very same emotions.*

Volunteer a personal story where you were also apprehensive about a new situation. Remind your son or daughter of the exciting times ahead, and that fresh starts allow us to break away from the limitations of old labels and past stereotypes. Assure your student that he/she will find that he/she has a lot of things in common with other students...the first being that they all chose the same school!

✶ The best way to make a friend is to be a friend.
Encourage your teenager to say "hi" to people he/she passes in the dorm that he/she hasn't met; encourage your student to talk to people in class; encourage your son or daughter to be involved. Doing things such as this will help provide the opportunity to meet new people and, perhaps, the chance to make a great friend.

It's normal to be nervous and apprehensive regarding the unknown. *Just make sure that your teenager doesn't turn that nervous energy into self-doubt.* Your student worked hard to get to this exciting point, so don't let apprehension paralyze him/her.

<u>*Words to pass on...*</u>

*F**ear is overcome by taking action!***

*Y**ou cannot climb the ladder of success
with your hands in your pockets.***

*I**t is not the situation,
but the way we respond to
the situation that's important.***

25. Roommate conflicts:
helping deal with poor matches.

Sometimes, roommate situations are known to get a little tense. Sometimes they can even get downright volcanic. It's easy to understand why. Shared rooms, limited privacy, the pressures of school...if this isn't a training ground for learning to get along with others in life, nothing is.

When problems do arise between roommates, not every teenager is prepared to handle them. The first reaction of many young people thrust into this situation is to throw their arms in the air and complain. The second reaction is to "go to war." Neither response is beneficial to your student's mental health, therefore, a few suggestions could be helpful:

1. Don't make hasty judgments.
Snap judgments regarding a new roommate can often dictate the course of the relationship for the rest of the year. During the first few weeks, it's easy to notice the negatives rather than the positives. Tell your teenager to be patient and to get to know his/her roommate before casting an opinion. *Advise your student to worry about being a good roommate before he/she starts complaining about what a bad roommate he/she was stuck with.*

2. Talk it out.
If things don't improve after a few weeks, encourage your student to initiate a "roommate chat." Best if conducted on neutral ground (i.e., a coffee shop, the cafeteria, etc.), advise your teenager to sensitively broach the subject of the irritants that have arisen. Your student will probably find that his/her roommate has been bothered by a few things as well. If your student is timid about a face-to-face meeting, perhaps he/she can write his/her thoughts on paper. *Stress the importance that neither the "chat" nor the note should be confrontational.* Going on the offensive (or the defensive) can bring disastrous results.

3. Compromise.
Sure, the stress of school sometimes causes one roommate to take frustrations out on the other, but this doesn't mean that things can't be worked out. The best thing to do is to encourage your student to be patient and to take the time to work things through with his/her roommate.

If a point arises that neither your student nor his/her roommate can agree upon, encourage your son or daughter to seek a compromise. *Winning an argument isn't what is important; finding a winning solution to which both parties can agree is.* Short term victories by one roommate can lead to bitterness from the other. It is best to reach a mutually agreed upon decision where both roommates win.

4. If living in the dorms, seek staff help.
If trying to talk it out doesn't work, recommend seeking help from a resident staff member. Serving as a mediator, residential staff members are trained to handle roommate

problems. After hearing both sides, staff members bring a third party perspective that often sheds light on a deteriorating situation. Formal lines are then drawn to prevent the situations from reoccurring.

5. The last resort...find a new roommate.

Unfortunately, there are a few matches that just don't work. If your student happens to be in one of those matches, it might be best to get a new roommate. If your student is living in the dorms, he/she will probably have to wait until the end of the semester. Residential staff are usually reluctant to make roommate changes unless things get really bad, and then it depends upon the availability of an alternate room in which to switch your student.

Before this final solution is deemed necessary, remind your teenager that *nothing guarantees that a new roommate will be any better.* The only thing that it does guarantee is that two (or more) people will have to begin from step one the whole process of adjusting to living together. For those who live off-campus, it means either locating a new apartment or going through the hassle of finding a new roommate.

In the end, your teenager's roommate situation can have a dramatic effect on the quality of the school year. Listen closely to what your son or daughter says about the situation, and offer input where needed.

<u>*Words to pass on...*</u>

A friendly voice can go a long way in solving the worst of conflicts.

To get an idea accepted, use a flyrod not a feeding tube.

26. Roommates:
helping fill out a roommate selection card.

Good or bad, roommates can set the tone for the year. Nobody wants the roommate from hell, but somebody will get him or her. *Your student increases his odds of being that person if he/she doesn't take the time to think about what he/she wants in a roommate.*

It's an understatement to say that filling out a roommate selection card is important. If your student takes the time to answer the questions thoughtfully, honestly, and as completely as possible, he/she significantly increases his/her chances of getting a compatible roommate. If there was ever a moment you should review your student's work, now is the time. This little exercise is simply too important to take lightly.

Here are a few issues that have the potential to make your student's roommate situation uncomfortable. To avoid trouble in the long run, make sure that your son or daughter responds thoughtfully to these areas now; they could end up being the difference between a well-matched roommate and a poorly matched roommate.

1. Cleanliness...
Coming back to the dorm every day to a messy room can be

very irritating to a neat person. Likewise, if your son or daughter is a little lazy in keeping the room picked up, your student can be sure that a "neat freak" roommate will only put up with so much before starting World War III. This is a good area to emphasize on your student's card. Merely checking the "neatness" box will probably get little attention.

2. Sleeping hours...

An "early bird" can count on clashing "big time" with a person who enjoys sleeping late. A bad way for anybody to start a morning is by entering into a shouting match. If this is an area that is important to your son or daughter, then encourage him/her to highlight this on the roommate selection card.

3. Study habits...

Some students like to study in their room. Other students like to have friends over and play music loudly. This is a sure indication of a bad roommate match, and a red flag for poor grades.

4. Music tastes...

Country music lovers and rappers are about as compatible as hard rockers and classical enthusiasts. To many students, perhaps yours, music is important. If this is an area where your student has strong tastes, it is highly advisable to list this on the roommate selection card. Dueling stereos are never recommended.

5. Hobbies and interests...

Having a roommate that your son or daughter enjoys doing things with is certainly an added bonus. Although it's not a necessity to be best pals, having a roommate who shares a common love of sports or, perhaps, the same career interest (i.e., teaching, business, etc.) can really make the year more enjoyable. If your student has strong passions in regard to a hobby or outside interest, or a strong distaste as well, he/she might want to stress this when filling out his/her card or packet.

6. Selecting the room size...

Some dorms also have rooms that are triples or suites. In order to save money on housing, your student might opt to go this direction. Having two (or more) roommates instead of one can be either a lot of fun or nothing short of a disaster.

In triples, the rooms aren't much larger than a double, so things are very tight. Neatness becomes a predominant issue. Students that live in triples are apt to spend more time away from their room than someone living in a double, so the saving of housing money needs to be weighed with the potential negatives.

7. Choosing a specific person...

If your student plans to room with a "friend from home," make sure that he/she understands that this can sometimes be hazardous to a relationship. Sure it seems like a lot of fun to room with a buddy; however, the level of comfort that exists between the two does not necessarily mean that they will make great roommates. Advise your son or daughter to think carefully about making the decision to do this.

Of course, it's impossible for your son or daughter to screen him/herself from every single annoying or dissimilar habit. Regardless of whom your student is matched up with, something will inevitably come up. *However, big problems (and the "roommate from hell") can be avoided if your student takes the time to fill out his/her card thoroughly.*

Words to pass on...

It is easier to get a good roommate when one is a good roommate.

27. Sexual harassment:
helping your teenager handle the situation.

Sexual discrimination happens. So does sexual harassment. There are no reasons that either should be tolerated. Certainly, the social conscience has reached an all-time high regarding these areas, but that does not mean, however, that incidents still do not occur.

You have probably had a talk or two on this subject with your teenager already. No doubt, it is a good idea to be repetitious and go over the subject one more time before your student leaves for college. Share with your teenager the three strike system:

1. Strike one...

If a comment is made that is sexually discriminating or harassing, advise your student to speak up in the boldest possible way. There is no justification to accept the comment or situation. Zero. Tell your teenager to inform the offending party (i.e., professor, fellow student, campus employee) that his/her comments are offensive and sexually harassing (or discriminating). That sort of boldness will usually cause the offender to be very careful about what is said to your student in the future.

2. Strike two...

If in the future this behavior does continue, however, it is time to address the issue by contacting (writing or calling) a higher authority within the college. Contact the Department Chair or Dean. Contact the Housing manager. Contact the college President's office. Take action.

3. Strike three!

If your student's efforts have fallen on deaf ears, it's time to strongly consider legal recourse. Of course, this final alternative should be thoroughly considered before a decision is made to take it. If, however, the situation is serious (i.e., your student's grade is being held over his/her head), nothing less than taking legal action will suffice.

On the subject of rape...

It is common knowledge that rape is one of the fastest growing crimes of violence in the country. Very few issues should be taken as seriously as the issue of rape. As your teenager heads off to college, there is one message that needs to be hammered home regarding this subject...*always be aware.*

✶ Be aware on campus.

Many places on campus are dark and not well lighted. Some heavily landscaped areas are particularly dangerous and serve as prime locations for rapes to occur. Avoid both of these areas.

Additionally, persuade your son or daughter of the importance of never walking alone at night. Whether it be returning from an evening lecture or from studying in the library, there is never a reason to walk by oneself. If a friend is not available to walk with him/her, tell your student to call campus security and wait until they come. *Carrying a whistle, pepper spray or some other preventative item is a very good idea.*

＊ **Be aware in social situations.**
Even if your student believes that he/she knows the person, he/she should still be on his/her guard. It's a pathetic statement on our society, but it is reality. *Rapes usually occur by someone we know.*

Remind your son or daughter to stay in control of all social situations. Recommend that he/she gets in the habit of leaving detailed notes for a roommate telling where he/she is going and when he/she will return. If he/she is going to be late, tell your student to call and leave a message. And one final note...always limit the alcohol.

Words to pass on...

There is never a bad time to exercise good judgment.

28. Medical emergencies:
<u>*preparing your son/daughter*</u>
<u>*for emergencies.*</u>

Among the many issues that you will be addressing with your student before he/she leaves for college, medical coverage should be a top priority. *Would your teenager know what to do if his/her roommate collapsed? Would he/she be able to handle a medical emergency? If your student was in an accident, would your insurance cover him/her?*

Whether it's simply having the phone number of the campus medical facility or knowing how to administer mouth-to-mouth resuscitation to someone who has stopped breathing, *your teenager should be prepared to handle emergency situations.* It could mean the difference between life and death.

Here are a few items that should be addressed with the utmost diligence:

1. Make sure that your teenager has medical coverage.
✶ Basic student health coverage...
Provided at minimal cost to students, most universities and

colleges offer quality health care services. First-aid treatment, x-rays, medicines, diagnostic tests, and counseling services are a part of the typical treatment offered. In the case of surgery, hospitalization, treatment of more extreme health care problems, or for out-of-town medical attention, additional insurance is probably required.

✶ Supplementary student health coverage...

The college probably has a supplemental policy in which your student can enroll. Usually offered at lower rates, this supplemental plan might provide the additional coverage that your student needs. Evaluate and compare the college policy's merits and costs with the coverage that your teenager qualifies for under your current plan.

2. Make sure that your student is prepared to handle an emergency.

✶ Training...

Your teenager should receive professional training in first-aid techniques, including CPR. Knowledge of what to do while waiting for emergency help to arrive can be crucial in determining the outcome of the emergency situation.

✶ Resources...

Upon your student's arrival at college, *follow up to make certain that he/she not only knows where the medical facilities are located, but also that your teenager has written down the phone numbers of these facilities.* Advise your student to keep one list posted in his/her room and another in his/her wallet. Also, *all college bound students should receive a first-aid kit and a medical handbook when leaving home.* Make sure that your teenager knows how to use both.

116

3. A note on dental care...

Dental insurance is probably not covered by the college's health plan. That doesn't mean, however, that periodic check-ups and cleanings should be missed. Of course, your student can continue to receive care from his/her current dentist when he/she comes home for break. Otherwise, you should direct your student to contact campus health services for local referrals who might provide routine cleanings at discounted prices to students. Additionally, if the college has a dental school on campus, your student will find that he/she can receive superb treatment for minimal charges.

Words to pass on...

T he first step in performing well in an emergency is knowing how to respond in an emergency.

29. Money 101:
checking accounts, credit cards and budgets.

Money management is definitely not a skill that a majority of college bound freshmen have mastered. They haven't had to. While living under your roof, your student has probably been shielded from experiencing the financial stress of paying "incidentals" like the mortgage (rent), food, utilities, insurance, etc. The transition to college, however, marks the beginning of some new understandings. One of the first is the issue of money.

The difference in having to find the money to pay for a couple of fast food hamburgers in high school to needing to pay for college text books can be a major paradigm shift for any teenager. As shocking as it may be to your student, it is a very healthy lesson to learn. *The transition from dependent living to independent living has begun.*

Money 101 begins with your student opening a checking account. It progresses into teaching credit card responsibility. The difficulty of this course is that although there is a professor (you), it is strictly "hands on." Learning how to make ends meet by setting up and living under a budget is one of the unique college courses that doesn't show up on the official transcript. The classroom is real life, and a bad grade in this class leads to real problems. This is why you need to spend time with your teenager before he/she leaves for college and teach him/her the "secrets" of money management and budgeting.

1. Checking Accounts.

✶ Establish a local account.

Cashing out of town checks sometimes presents inconveniences. For understandable reasons, many merchants around college communities are sometimes reluctant to cash or even accept them. Because of this, *it is more convenient for your student to establish a checking account in the local community.*

If there is not a local branch of your home bank, recommend that your son or daughter contact the banks around campus. Advise him/her to make a selection based on criteria such as monthly checking fees and services offered. More than likely, the bank provides a special service for student accounts.

✶ Follow check writing guidelines.

Before your student gets to the point of writing checks, here are a few parameters that you can go over with him/her that will save both of you a few headaches later:

(1) Keep the checkbook register up to date every time a check is written.

(2) Double check the figures.

(3) Hang on to deposit slips until they appear on the monthly statement.

(4) **Reconcile the checkbook when the monthly statement is delivered.**

(5) **Hang on to canceled checks as proof of payment.**

(6) **Never write a check for more than is available in the account; bounced checks lead to added fees.**

2. Credit Cards.

* **A careful decision.**

Before you help your student get a credit card, give the subject serious thought. Of course, your teenager will be fond of the idea. Coffee shops, restaurants, campus clothing shops, flower shops, shoe stores, concerts...the possibilities are numerous.

Although it may be convenient for your student, having a credit card brings substantial risks. Unlike check writing that gives a buyer a running total of money spent versus money in the account, credit card expenditures always seem to come as a surprise when monthly statements arrive. The only accountability factor built into credit card usage is the pre-determined spending limit.

* **A credit card can be a useful tool if used responsibly.**
If you do decide to set a credit card account up, consider adding a few additional restrictions so that surprises and risks are minimized. Here are a few guidelines:

(1) **Apply for a card with a limit that you set, not the company.**

(2) **Establish boundaries with your student on how the card is to be used.**

(3) **Stay on top of things. Make sure that you review the monthly statement.**

(4) Pay the whole bill every month. Do not make interest only payments.

(5) Make sure that your son or daughter keeps all receipts.

(6) If things don't work out, cancel the card.

3. Living under a budget.
✳ Learning fiscal responsibility.

Regardless of whether or not finances are tight, be adamant about your college student developing and living under a budget. If you are contributing financially to your son or daughter's education, fiscal responsibility is one of those subjects where the professorial duties fall to you. Therefore, do not neglect the importance of educating your student in the finer art of budgeting.

✳ Determine the amount of money that will be needed.

In building a budget, one of the first things that your son or daughter will need to do is to determine exactly how much money will be needed to cover everything. The college or university that your freshman will be attending will be able to provide the needed costs for the majority of these areas (tuition, room and board, etc.).

Budget categories such as transportation, clothing, telephone, and discretionary spending are more personal. You and your student will have to make the determination as to how much should be spent in these areas.

Here are the top ten budget items that should be accounted for:

(1) Tuition.

(2) Room and board.

(3) Books and supplies.

(4) Insurance (medical, auto).

(5) Fees (activity card, drop/add fees, lab fees).

(6) Transportation.

(7) Telephone.

(8) Fraternity or sorority dues.

(9) Discretionary spending.

(10) Personal expenses (clothing, laundry, bathroom items, etc.).

✷ **Make sure that funds set aside for college equal budget demands.**

After determining a specific amount for each budget item, you will then know how much money will be needed to cover first year expenses. By now, your family probably has a good idea of how to pay for college. A combination of sources including grants, loans, scholarships, and family and student earnings will surely be needed. *The specific amount that will be received from each source should be known.*

Obviously, if expenses exceed income, there is a problem. If this happens, your family should discuss each of the individual sources from which your student is receiving money, and then decide from which area funds can be increased (greater family contribution, increased work hours for the student, another loan, etc.). Helping make the necessary adjustments now will avoid big problems later.

4. Sticking to a budget.

✶ Setting priorities.

Make sure that the money needed for tuition and room and board is set aside immediately. Fees, insurance and books need to be the next priority. As for the more individualized expenses (trips home, clothing, laundry, bathroom items, telephone, and discretionary spending), your student will need to allocate specific amounts in which he/she will not exceed in spending each month (i.e., telephone $30, pizza money $20).

The power of living within a budget is that expenses are rarely a surprise and unnecessary spending is kept to a minimum. *Living within a budget assures your student that expenses will not surpass income.*

✶ Tips that can help your student keep expenses down:

(1) Graduate on time.

Reduce the time it takes to finish the degree. Set a goal of four years and not five years. That extra year means thousands of dollars in additional expenses.

(2) Say "No!"

Remind your student to buy only what he/she needs. Joining the gang and chipping in for a late night pizza can begin to take a toll on the checkbook.

(3) Save on books.

- If a professor only recommends a book, your student might not need to buy it.

- Sell books back at the end of the semester.
- Check the library to see if the professor has put any copies on reserve.
- Tell your student to buy used books and to watch bulletin boards for trades.

(4) Use the mail.
Letters are cheaper than the phone.

A special note regarding debt...

Some parents question whether or not they should allow their students, or themselves, to go into debt by paying for college. Certainly, the fear of debt is not for everyone, but if college dreams would otherwise be extinguished by not taking out the necessary loans, then forget it! *Keep borrowing in perspective, but encourage your student to do what it takes to make getting a college education possible.*

<u>*Words to pass on...*</u>

*There is a sure fire way to double your money...
fold it in half and put it in your pocket.*

30. Transportation:
Cars, bikes, and public possibilities.

The transportation issue is certainly not one in which parents are unfamiliar. In the early years, it was figuring out a "shuttle" schedule for Little League and dance practices. When your student reached the driving age, the transportation worries took on an element of nervous concern as your teen hit the highways for the first time. For many parents, the transportation saga continues when their son or daughter heads off to college.

As you may have already discovered, the issue of taking a car to college has the potential of being a very divisive issue between parents and students. Emotional arguments aside, let's look at the pros and cons of taking a car to college, as well as the pros and cons connected to a few other popular modes of transportation:

1. The car...leaving with it or living without it.
The decision of whether or not to allow your son or daughter to take a car to college should be done with great delib-eration. Certainly, individual circumstances make all the difference. Use the following list to help you evaluate the merits of both sides:

125

✶ The reasons pointing to leaving the car at home...

(1) Increased expenses (operating costs, insurance, parking permits, tickets).

(2) Friends borrowing it.

(3) Temptation of drinking and driving.

(4) Increased opportunities for theft and vandalism.

(5) The availability of public transportation.

✶ The reasons pointing to taking the car...

(1) Greater flexibility.

(2) Makes grocery shopping and getting to class easier for those living off campus.

(3) Transportation to come home on weekends, holidays and other breaks.

2. To bike or not to bike...

Bicycles can be a convenient form of transportation on many campuses. On other campuses, the value of having a bike is diminished by the problems of storage and theft. Before your teenager makes a decision, *recommend that he/she wait for a few weeks until he/she knows exactly what his/her personal needs will be.*

✶ Be safe and buy used.

If your student decides that he/she needs a bike, *make sure that he/she gets a good lock and registers the bike with the campus police.* Additionally, have him/her consider buying a used bike rather than going through the hassle of bringing one from home. Ads for inexpensive bikes can often be found on student bulletin boards or the school paper. Sure, the bike might not be the most glamorous, but why risk the threat of having an expensive bike stolen?

126

3. Other options...

✳ Use public transportation.

If your student lives off campus, public buses and subways can certainly help your student get to and from class. Public transportation is a viable option. Although it isn't as convenient for your student as having his/her own car, routes are usually regular and on time. Additionally, there aren't any parking or parking fee worries. Advise your student to get a schedule of route times and give it a try.

✳ Share a ride home.

To find a ride home, suggest that your student post something in the dorm, the sorority or the fraternity. The campus Ride Board might also have a few possibilities, but remind your son or daughter to go into those situations a little more guarded. *At large campuses, finding another student that is traveling across state or across the country is pretty common.* Splitting gas money for a ride home benefits both students.

<u>Words to pass on...</u>

The most popular kid on the dorm floor is the one with the car.

A blessing once believed is often a headache soon realized.

A time to support... family changes.

31. Changes:
<u>dealing with changes in appearance, beliefs and attitudes:</u>

The first year of college can push freshman off balance. New freedoms and a search for an adult identity can lead students to respond and change in a number of ways. You might find many of these behavioral changes surprising. You also may discover that they don't meet your approval.

Marked by self-doubt, this period of "finding one's self" can be a real testing ground for your student. Changes can range from simply being more aggressive in vocalizing political beliefs to completely disregarding previous values regarding drinking and sex. been "experimenting" with marijuana.

What do these changes mean? What is really happening? College is a time that young people challenge their parents' beliefs. Now that they are on their own, students have the opportunity to push past the rules that they grew up with and either accept or reject the values you taught. *For many, it is a time of breaking loose and trying new things.*

<u>Potential changes could include...</u>

1. A change in attitude.

2. A change in appearance.

3. A change in political or religious beliefs.

4. A change in values or lifestyle.

Of course, there is the strong possibility that positive changes could also emerge. Maybe a year away from home could foster a more sensitive, mature and appreciative attitude on the part of your student. In that case, count your blessings. However, if your student's behavior falls well short of your desired plan, here are a few tips:

1. Listen with an open mind.

Your son or daughter's exposure to new people and different experiences is more than likely going to stimulate new ideas. Some of these ideas might catch you a bit off-guard. Nonetheless, *it is important to keep communication open, and being quick to judge will only shut the door on communication.* Be sensitive and listen.

2. Give advice...lightly.

Until you fully understand the reasons behind the change in your son or daughter's behavior, your best course of action is to stay away from giving advice. *Before you say something that you'll regret, make sure that you comprehend the situation completely.* Think through exactly what you want to say before you open your mouth. The fastest horse can't catch a word spoken in anger.

Whatever you do, don't argue! *Arguing and verbally striking out will put both you and your teenager in a defensive position.* This sort of negative communication is not conducive to establishing the sort of dialogue that can potentially help put your son or daughter back on track.

3. Explain the potential consequences of this particular action or decision.

After thoroughly thinking through the situation, explain to your teenager that you are confused by his/her behavior. Clear the air and, in a very calm and deliberate manner, let him/her know how you feel about the changes that you are seeing.

Discuss the possible consequences that could come as a result of your student making this particular decision. Explore together how his/her decision or actions might affect other family members or, perhaps, his/her own future opportunities (i.e., employment).

If you find that that your student's behavior is completely reprehensible and totally void of the values to which you prescribe, be honest and tell him/her. *Make sure that you communicate with as much love as possible*, but anything less than 100% honest communication will be a disservice to your son or daughter in the long run.

4. Show concrete signs of your support and love.

During this period of change, it is important to share with
your student that you love him/her. Besides verbally ex-
pressing this, there are other things that you can do to
show that you care. Visiting him/her at school and sending letters, care packages and clippings from the hometown newspaper are a few examples.

Additionally, take an interest in his/her academic and social
life. Ask to read the papers that he/she has written. Praise
and encourage his/her work, but don't criticize it. You
have a higher calling than serving as an armchair professor; *your number one objective is to build a bond that*
can help your student get through a tough time.

5. Seek professionals for help when necessary.

If the changes that your student is going through start to get
serious, consider contacting professionals that can lend
support and advice. Constructive feedback from members of the health and religious fields can help you re-
solve and understand the prominent issues that are moti-
vating your student's erratic and negative behavior.

Your life is probably different since your freshman left home,
so don't be surprised if you are thrown off balance by having
to deal with the changes your teenager is experiencing. It
might be hard, but you need to step back into full-time parent
mode. *Your teenager needs your support and guidance*
through this troubling time of finding an adult identity.

Words to pass on...

*T*he starting point for both success and
happiness is a healthy self-image.

*"I*n reading the lives of great people, I found
that the first victory they won
was over themselves . . .
self-discipline with all of them came first."
- Harry S. Truman

32. Drinking:
dealing with the issue of alcohol and drugs.

Alcohol and drugs are prevalent on college campuses. Certainly, they are also a part of the high school scene, but the big difference now is their everyday availability and the lack of immediate consequences of imbibing. The fear of coming home from a high school party blasted and confronting an irate parent is much different from being laughed at by a roommate. Not having to answer to a parent figure makes it that much easier to have an extra beer...or two...or three.

1. A time of experimentation...
Of course, all parents would like to believe that their student can handle both the peer pressure and the temptation of picking up that first drink. *The reality is, however, most students do try alcohol.* Parents who ascribe to the belief that their son or daughter will be the one who won't are only fooling themselves.

It is true that students today are more aware of the danger and addictive nature of drugs than in years past. This does not mean, however, that the availability of certain drugs, like marijuana and cocaine, has decreased. To the contrary, certain drugs are widely popular and readily available. The most common of all is alcohol.

2. A time of vulnerability...

College parties notoriously revolve around alcohol, and freshman are particularly vulnerable to its perceived benefits. The tensions associated with difficult educational demands, changing environments, and trying to fit in drive thousands of college students to take a stronger interest in "social drinking." Helping your student differentiate between what is social drinking and what is alcohol abuse falls under your parental umbrella.

* **Stress responsibility and safety.**
Anyone can become a victim of drug or alcohol abuse...including your student. Abuse can range from needing a drink to feel social to missing class because of having drank too much the night before. Separated by distance, you need to strongly convey the overwhelming downside of drugs and alcohol before your student leaves home.

3. A time of self-control...

Failing to give suggestions to your son or daughter regarding how to handle possible scenarios is leaving him/her open to the possibility of falling into a situation that he/she would rather avoid. As simple as the choices are, do not assume that your student has their act together in this area. *Help your son or daughter explore the different options that are available when he or she comes face to face with a fraternity keg:*

* **If your student is committed to staying away from alcohol...**
(1) Strongly encourage him/her to stay away from parties where alcohol is served, especially parties where getting drunk is the top objective.

(2) Suggest that your student seek out social circles where alcohol is not the center of attention. Involvement in campus organizations and church groups is an option.

(3) Encourage the planning of weekend activities with friends ahead of time in order to avoid having nothing to do on Friday night, except go to the beer bash.

✶ **If your student does want to go to the party and would like to limit drinking...**

(1) Encourage your student to tell others that he/she doesn't drink. It's really not that big a deal that he/she doesn't, and self-control is an admirable quality.

(2) Encourage him/her to drink a soda, water, or some other non-alcoholic beverage. Pouring the drink into a cup prevents others from knowing what he/she is drinking.

(3) If your student wants to drink, suggest nursing the same drink for the night.

(4) Recommend that he/she go to the party with a light or non-drinking friend who can hold him/her accountable for how much he/she drinks.

(5) Advise your student that when he/she starts to feel the effects of the alcohol, that is a warning signal to either stop drinking or to go home. Do not wait until he/she starts experiencing a loss of tongue, mind, or body control.

✶ **If you fear that your student is vulnerable to alcohol and drugs...**

(1) In the strongest possible way, remind your student of the

potential consequences of drinking and using drugs. Besides the health risks, other potential consequences include being kicked out of the dorms, expulsion from school, and possible criminal charges.

(2) If you realize that your son or daughter already has a problem, you need to demand that he/she seek immediate professional help. If this means missing a semester, so be it. If you don't hold your student accountable, who will? This is one issue that your teenager should not feel is open for debate with you.

When the alcohol flows freely, trouble often follows. *Tell your student that maturity means having the strength of character to say no to drinking and drug use.* Encourage your son or daughter to choose a different and wiser path than some of his/her peers. In the end, your student will have far fewer regrets.

Words to pass on...

*C**haracter is much easier kept than recovered.*

33. Transfering colleges:
considering the option.

Sometimes, the expectations that a student has for a particular college are not met. Perhaps a specialized area of study proved to be weaker than expected, or the faculty credentials at another college are stronger. Maybe a change in a family's financial situation has caused a public university to be more attractive than the currently attended private one. Perhaps the desire to attend college in a warm climate is more important than expected, or a longing to study at a smaller university becomes paramount.

Whether it be academic, financial, social, or emotional, the reasons for desiring to transfer to another college are as diverse as the students themselves. If your student falls into one of these categories and proves to be unhappy with the college that he/she is currently attending, obviously, you should be concerned.

Assuming that a great deal of consideration went into the initial selection, a decision to transfer colleges should not be taken lightly. Here are a few guidelines that could help when you get a rather "interesting" phone call from your son or daughter.

1. Address the subject...now.

If your son or daughter mentions a desire to transfer colleges, inquire as to the reason immediately. Do not let this particular subject slide by without getting deeper insight as to why your student is even considering the option.

Although your first reaction might be to become upset, catch yourself. At this point, listening will serve a greater purpose in the long run than "dictating." *Find out what the issues are and strongly encourage your student to wait a couple of months before making any hasty decisions.* Depending on the urgency, you might need to make the effort to meet in person.

2. Make sure that the desire to transfer is for the right reasons.

There are legitimate reasons to transfer colleges, and then there are reasons not so legitimate. Being homesick or missing a boyfriend or girlfriend doesn't carry as much weight as desiring a college with a stronger engineering program. *Direct your son or daughter to make this particular decision based on the head and not the heart.* Redirect his/her attention to the "big picture" and not just the moment.

3. Understand the consequences of transferring.

Because not all classes are transferred equally between colleges, your student risks the possibility of losing credits. This means possibly lengthening the amount of time that it will take to finish the degree.

4. Be familiar with the new college.
Advise your student to be fully aware of the transfer and degree requirements at the new college. Have your student talk with the admissions staff before making any final decisions. Sending an unofficial copy of a transcript to the desired college might give your student a better idea of what classes will transfer and what classes won't transfer.

If the motivation for transferring is based on reasons other than academic, financial, or location, make sure that the same problems won't occur again at the new college. The cost of time and money is too great to experience this process too many times.

5. Before your student drops out, make sure that he/she is accepted.
Make sure that your student doesn't automatically assume that he/she will be accepted at the new college. *Suggest taking a leave of absence from the current college instead of withdrawing altogether.* Securing the current college as a backup is much better than having no alternative if a rejection letter comes in the mail.

6. Transfer in the fall.
Transferring at the beginning of the academic year might not make a difference academically, but it can make a difference socially. Making friends and "fitting in" is easier when other people are making the adjustment to a new environment as well.

A special note regarding transfers from a junior college...

It's not uncommon for a junior college transfer to feel alone at the new campus. If your transfer student feels "awkward" about hanging out with incoming freshman, or if he/she feels unwelcome by students who have already been attending, advise him/her to get over it. The quality of his/her new relationships at school will directly correspond with the amount of effort he/she is willing to put into developing them. *Strongly encourage your junior transfer to find activities and organizations of interest and become involved.*

Words to pass on...

*T*he difference between "wanting to transfer" and "wanting to stay" is sometimes one more semester.

34. Dropping out:
dealing with a desire to leave school.

Unfortunately, not every incoming freshman will make it through the first year of college. A number of students will be motivated to withdraw because of homesickness, academic difficulty, social pressures, or perhaps even a boyfriend or girlfriend back home. Hopefully, none of these "inducements" will befall your student.

When things don't go as planned, it's easy for your student to start thinking about the comforts of home. With finals approaching and grades already teetering on the edge, thoughts of how easy it was at home last summer become rather comforting. Your student starts to wonder if he/she is up to the task of going to college at all. "Maybe I should take some time off and decide what I really want to do?" This is the beginning of a parent four-alarm-alert!

Dropping out of school without finishing the year is not the best idea. The early stages of entering the drifting zone can be dangerous. For some students, dropping out early marks the beginning of a period of wandering. With limited purpose and accountability, some dropouts begin the process of going from one thing to another with restrained commitment. Other students who skip a year don't go back. Earning money, acquiring possessions, and paying bills all create roadblocks in finding the way back to the classroom.

If you find yourself in the position of discussing the subject of dropping out with your student, you have good reason to worry. This is a very sensitive time and it requires your greatest parental skills. *Now, as much as ever, your son or daughter's future relies on your ability to diplomatically motivate your student to stay the course.*

Here are a few principles that could help guide your strategy in dealing with a student interested in dropping out:

1. Convince your student not to do anything radical.

Once one's perspective gets out of control, it's hard to look beyond the situation immediately at hand. Hopefully, your son or daughter will mention the subject of dropping out before he/she actually does drop out.

If you know that your student is considering the idea, *strongly encourage him/her to stay the course until at least the semester break.* At that time, the two (or three) of you can get together and go over everything that is bothering your student. If your student is ready to walk out the door now, you need to discover the root of his/her motivation as soon as possible. Make whatever sacrifice is necessary and get together with your student immediately.

2. Ask your son or daughter the hard questions.

If your student is going to drop out, what is he/she going to do? Does he/she have a plan? If he/she doesn't feel ready for college now, what does he/she think will make him/her feel ready for college later? If he/she needs to "find him/herself," is he/she going to work? Is he/she going to travel? How is he/she going to support him/herself?

If your son or daughter decides to follow through with the decision to drop out, this might be the right time to let your teenager fly solo money wise. Help your student to see the potential consequences of his/her decision. Break down the emotion of the situation into the hard facts of the situation. *By helping your student see the complete picture, you are giving him/her the opportunity to make the right decision.*

3. Encourage your student to seek campus support.

If your student is struggling, encourage him/her to seek campus support. If the root of the problem is academic, tutoring might help your student regain his/her confidence. If he/she is having difficulty managing his/her time, or if he/she is not handling stress well, the career counseling center could provide invaluable assistance. If your student feels alone, push him/her to become involved in campus or local activities.

By making the commitment to do something, your student is taking the first step to feeling more comfortable about his/her particular situation. When his/her environment begins to feel more comfortable, your student will have less desire to drop out.

4. Stay in touch...constantly.

During this tenuous time, it is important that you talk with your student as much as possible. Show your love and support, and keep a finger on the pulse of the situation.

By keeping in close contact, you will be able to provide regular encouragement and, hopefully, be able to intervene before careless and unthinking decisions are made.

Don't let homesickness exaggerate your student's feeling of how "terrible" college is. Although you might feel it to be a compliment, don't let your student blow up out of proportion how great it would be to be at home. The fact is, *it is in his/her best interest to start making the physical and mental adjustments that are necessary to live independently.* Dropping out of college is definitely not a step in the right direction.

Feeling nervous and apprehensive about college and the future is normal. All students have a fear of not being able to handle college to some degree. It is when this fear is exaggerated that problems begin to build. Advise your student to take a step back and examine the big picture. *Taking a year off might not be career threatening for your student, but not getting a college degree at all could be.*

<u>*Words to pass on...*</u>

*F ear defeats more people
than any other one thing in the world.*

*"H alf the failures in life arise from pulling
in one's horse as he is leaping."
- Julius Charles Hare*

35. Staying in touch:
ways to stay close.

More than likely, your motivation for staying in close contact with your son or daughter is very high. For most families, their college bound student will no longer be living under the same roof. *This transition can be emotionally taxing on both you and your student.*

If you are not very good about staying in touch, *establish a commitment to follow through and communicate with your student at least on a weekly basis.* Regular communication is not only bond building, it is crucial in helping your son or daughter adjust to his or her new environment. Good intentions to stay close just don't cut it. There is no commitment more important than taking the time to show your student that you care.

The first month of college will be the hardest for your student. Having his/her life thrown completely into the air, he/she will be grateful to find that not every thing in his/her life has changed. Your support and encouragement will be much appreciated. Two or three short calls a week for the first month might be very appropriate.

Here are a few ideas to add consistency and variety to your

communication:

1. Phone calls...

✶ Call often.

Establish regular phone call days and times (i.e., 6:00 p.m. Sunday and Wednesday) and then commit to the schedule.

✶ Surprise your student.

Pick up the phone for no other reason but to tell your freshman that you were thinking about him/her and just wanted to let him/her know.

✶ Make sure other members of the family are around.

By having other members of the family available, your student gets a chance to talk with everyone in the family.

✶ You call.

By initiating all scheduled phone conversations, you remove your student's worry of having to pay for the long distance charges.

2. Letters...

✶ Letters from you.

Let your son or daughter know how proud you are of him/her. Always make your notes cheerful and upbeat. Don't look at writing the letters as a chore, but rather an enjoyable exercise in creativity. Have some fun!

✶ Letters from the family.

Encourage other family members to write letters or have them each write a little tidbit in one family letter. You can even design the letter to look like a newsletter (The Anderson

Times) with each person writing his or her own column.
Include pictures, comic strips, or anything else that would
be entertaining for your student to read.

✶ Letters from others.
Seek out past teachers, coaches, scout leaders, club advisors,
neighbors, friends and anybody else whom you can think
of to write a letter. A short note from somebody whom
your son or daughter respected will be an appreciated
surprise.

✶ Creative letters.
Write to one of your son or daughter's favorite celebrities or
role models and politely request that he or she send a
motivational note to your student. A signed photo from a
role model can brighten any day. If your student is at-
tached to a family pet at home, be creative and write your
student a letter from the perspective of the pet.

3. Care packages...
Here are a few items that you could include:
* ✶ Cookies or a box of chocolate.
* ✶ Hometown clippings.
* ✶ Photographs.
* ✶ Small reminders of home.
* ✶ Motivational posters.
* ✶ Funny cartoons.
* ✶ Drawings from a sibling.
* ✶ Old and new pictures.
* ✶ A new CD or tape cassette.
* ✶ Bathroom and personal items.

✶ Funny and interesting articles.

✶ A few extra spending dollars.

4. Tape cassettes...

✶ Send a tape cassette in which the entire family participates in the recording. Ask members to describe their day and talk about things that have been happening. Record the family dinner conversation or just add to the tape a little bit every day.

5. Other gestures that would be appreciated...

✶ Send flowers.

✶ Make special days special (Valentine's Day, Easter, Birthday, etc.).

✶ Subscribe to the weekend edition of the hometown newspaper for your student.

✶ Send entertaining postcards that you find.

✶ Show that you are interested in what your son or daughter is doing at school. Ask your student to send copies of her work home.

One of life's great surprises is that when we do things for other people, we end up doing something for ourselves. As you take the time to support and enrich your son or daughter's life while he/she is at college, your life becomes more enriched in the process. Don't worry if your actions aren't reciprocated. Take satisfaction in knowing that you're being the best parent that you can be.

Words to pass on...

*"Life is a series of experiences,
each one of which makes us bigger..."
- Henry Ford*

*Friendship is like a bank account. You can't
continue to draw on it without making deposits.*

36. Campus visits:
visiting your son/daughter at school.

Visiting your student at college is an event that the entire family can enjoy. Younger brothers and sisters can walk the campus in awe. They will love visiting campus stores and feeling great pride in buying a sweatshirt picturing their older sibling's school logo.

You will feel a great sense of pride touring the campus and listening to the animated stories that your son or daughter tells regarding his/her early experiences. Your student can relish in the pride that you feel. *This can be a terrific bonding experience.*

On the other hand, visiting your college student can be equally disastrous. By making the trip without receiving the endorsement of your student, you have laid the groundwork for a less than optimistic weekend. Feeling put out, your son/daughter doesn't greet your visit with the enthusiasm you expected. He/she wins no votes for entertainer of the year, as his/her attitude for the entire visit is less than desirable.

Now that he/she has to entertain his/her parents, your freshman is none to pleased. After learning that he/she has no interest in introducing you to his/her new friends, you begin to argue. Of course, you've had about enough of this "new" attitude, so you remind him/her who is paying the bill for this "college holiday." For some reason spending $60 on the evening meal has never been so disagreeable. You promise yourself to avoid this unpleasant experience again.

The difference between these two scenarios is strictly agenda...yours vs. your student's. *Instead of traveling with the intention of "checking out" your investment, you should visit the campus with the purpose of showing support, love, and pride.* Nothing more. Anything more is a prescription for a major debacle.

Here are a few ideas that will help make your campus visit more rewarding for everybody:

1. Make sure it's convenient for your student.

First off, *visit your student only if he/she welcomes you to come.* Express to your student that you would like to plan a trip, but don't push it. It's great if he/she is excited about your visit, but if he/she isn't thrilled, don't worry about it. At a time when your student is trying to find his/her balance, a visit by you could serve to be unsettling. There will be plenty of time to visit later.

If your student does want you to visit, let him/her set the date. Don't push for coming on a big football game weekend (that might be reserved for the dorm gang) or on the day of any other major campus event. Do your best to work around his/her schedule.

2. Don't invade your student's territory.

While visiting, don't demand to meet your freshman's new friends. College students sometimes don't feel too com-

153

fortable showing off their parents, so don't take it personally. *If your student has a game plan for your visit, it's best to agree with it.* The game plan has probably been created to make him/her feel more comfortable.

Similarly, don't insist on visiting the fraternity or sorority either. Creating uncomfortable situations for your son or daughter so that you can feel more comfortable will not sit well with your student.

3. Listen...don't lecture.

The purpose of the trip is not to assert your parental "veto" authority regarding the decisions that your freshman has made. Rather, the purpose of your visit is to be able to share the exciting adventure that your student is now experiencing.

During the trip, hold your tongue. Don't judge or provide critical commentary of your student or his/her new environment. This is a time to accept your student as an adult and efforts to assert parental authority will not go over well.

If your student's passion light has been lit by a class that he/she has taken or an organization that he/she has joined, don't burst his/her bubble. Even if you're paying the price of admission for his/her "college ticket," don't get uptight because he/she has broken the family's party affiliation and become a Young Republican.

It's important to remember that your student is just trying to establish his/her own identity; therefore, don't be surprised by changes in attitude or interest. In fact, expect it. Your student might try to test his/her new "persona" out on your visit, so if you find his/her attitude or actions irritable, just listen...support...and tolerate. For now.

4. If you do meet the new people in your son or daughter's life...

Your teenager will probably experience the internal debate of whether or not he/she should introduce you to his/her friends. If he/she does happen to bestow that honor upon you, don't do anything to embarrass him/her. Although common sense would seem to dictate here, parents always seem to get this part wrong. Here are a few rules that should be carefully considered:

* **Never divulge information about your student ("At home, John used to...").**

* **Never divulge information about yourself ("When I was in college...")**

* **Don't learn everything you can about your son/ daughter's friend in one sitting.**

Unless your teenager will be living at home, you won't have the same luxury of knowing whom he/she will be "hanging out with" as you did in high school. If you disagree with your freshman's choice of friends, be careful not to vocalize your opinion (exceptions should be made if you're really nervous about a particular individual). Part of the problem might just be over-protection. *No parent wants their son or daughter to associate with the wrong people, but you need to begin to trust your freshman's judgment at some point.*

155

Words to pass on...

*"There is very little difference in people,
but that difference makes a big difference.
That little difference is attitude.
The big difference is whether
it is positive or negative."
—W. Clement Stone*

*Encouragement is as vital to the soul
as oxygen is to the body.*

37. Coming home:
holidays and other trips home.

Expecting your student's return home for the holidays to be a glorious, fun-filled time of family bonding and Kodak moments is a little unrealistic. As much as parents would like the vacation break of their freshman to be a signal of profound personal growth, wisdom and sensitivity, it's probably not going to happen. *Often, the best you can hope for is strictly to survive on talking terms.*

When your freshman comes home for the holiday, don't expect that things will be the same as it was prior to his/her departure; *be prepared for changes.* The new people, new experiences, and new surroundings in your student's life will bring about changes in how your student sees him/herself and his/her world.

A new living and learning environment that stresses greater independence will naturally dictate changes in your student, both mentally and emotionally. For many parents, these changes will be something to celebrate; for others, they will be something to guard against.

Hopefully, your student will return home with a new sense of maturity, parental respect, and responsibility. More than likely, however, your student will return home with a different and less desirable agenda. The following actions sum up a few possibilities:

1. Desires to be the center of attention.

Unlike high school where the teacher knew who he/she was, college has probably been a shock. Returning from an environment where he/she is identified by an ID number and has lecture classes larger than his/her graduating high school class, your student could choose to elevate him/herself to center stage upon returning home.

Prepared to share every experience and every bit of knowledge that he/she has gained, *your student monopolizes the moment in order to help combat internal insecurities.* Entering back into an environment that is comfortable, your student will love the special feeling that returning home brings.

2. Seeks to turn back the clock.

There is no doubt that some students will be thrilled to come home. The opportunity to escape the rigors of college and the demands of professors will assuredly bring a smile to their face. However, the opportunity to return to the less demanding comforts of home gives students a reason to celebrate!

Problems in this scenario arise when your student enjoys home too much and is unhappy about returning to college after the break. *If your freshman starts to talk negatively about college, be prepared to shift the conversation back to the positive.*

Keep the focus of the visit on the terrific opportunities that college brings. Suggest that your freshman return to his/her high school and volunteer information about college with others. Enter into stimulating conversations that allow your student the chance to feel good about what he/she is learning. Raise his/her self-esteem by giving him/her the opportunity to teach the family. If one of his/her new college friends lives nearby, encourage him/her to invite the friend over. *By concentrating on the things about college that make him/her feel positive, thoughts of how great the past was will hopefully disappear.*

3. Acts as if he/she is above it all.

Now that opinions have been given added substance, your student might try to show off his/her new knowledge base. With new perspectives regarding politics, religion, sex, and virtually every other subject, your student could approach his/her trip home believing he/she is now on a higher intellectual plane than other members of the family.

Unless you're humored by it, this new attitude (best described as cockiness) will probably not sit too well with you. Looking to test you out on controversial topics, your student will rebel against having the same rules at home that he/she had while in high school. If your student chooses this path, be prepared for clashes of the highest order!

5. Needs to express independence.

Vacations and breaks are often marked by power struggles. The college freshman believes that he/she shouldn't have rules to follow when he/she comes home. Parents believe that their way is always best and nothing that their son or daughter can say will get rid of the 11:00 p.m. curfew. So what do you do?

Certainly, you will be tempted to jump in and start directing the course of your student's life when he/she returns home. *If possible, try to avoid governing with an iron fist.*

If your student wants to spend time with friends while at home, let him/her. If he/she wants to stay out late, ask him/her to tell you what time would be reasonable to return home. Express that you feel comfortable with him/her making mature decisions; however, for safety reasons, you should still demand to know some specifics regarding the evening (i.e., times, places, people and phone numbers).

At this stage of the game, controlling your teenager doesn't go over too well. *If he/she wants to be independent, remember, it is his/her life.* Don't get your feelings hurt; just make sure to schedule specific time blocks in order to spend family time together. Likewise, as an adult, he/she should make sure to honor the time blocks that he/she does set with you and the rest of the family.

Realizing that the first few visits home by your student may not qualify your freshman as a role model, be patient. The truth is that unless you work at it, you might not make the cover of *Parenting Magazine* either. *Undoubtedly, this unique period in both of your lives represents a terrific opportunity to grow together.* It takes work, but a determined effort to work through this period constructively can pay dividends that last a lifetime.

<u>*Words to pass on...*</u>

*L*ife is an echo.
What you send out, you get back.
What you give, you get.

*P*eople don't care about
how much you know,
unless they know much much you care—
about them!

38. Family:
helping you and the young ones make the transition.

Every member of the family is affected when your college bound freshman leaves home. Siblings, moms and dads are all vulnerable to experiencing the emotional rollercoaster that inevitably comes when a family member heads off to college.

Although competition for the channel changer is now gone, an empty spot at the dinner table is not easily forgotten. Sure, the telephone doesn't ring as much and the music that plays on the stereo is quieter, but, somehow, those missing sounds seem to leave the house a little more solemn.

As difficult as it might be, it is important to help members of the family look at this period as one of potential growth and not loss. Overcoming separation anxiety is not easy, but the benefits of reaching a new level of understanding can make a huge difference in the quality and attitude of a family member's life. Helping those closest to you deal with the change should become a top priority when your college bound student leaves home.

162

Tips for younger siblings...

Separation is an ongoing process in life. As the family begins to disperse, changes in the family are inevitable. Milestones, like going to college, are a fact of life and, unfortunately, sadness does play a part in the change. Younger children remaining at home might not understand the transition taking place. In case they take this time especially hard, here are a few ideas to help make things easier.

1. Be positive.

Act confident about the changes so that your children at home will still feel confident and secure. By putting a positive spin on the situation, you help guide the attitude of young ones. Tell your youngster that what his big brother or sister is doing is really exciting and that he/she will have fun stories to tell about college. Challenge your youngster to start learning about lots of fun things that he/she can share also.

2. Be generous with your time.

Be sensitive to spend extra time with your youngster for at least the first few weeks of the new change. Read together. Play in the yard. Whether it be dinosaurs or super hero characters, totally involve yourself with activities that interest your youngster.

3. Be specific about the next visit.

Write on a calendar the next time that the youngster will be able to see his/her big brother or sister. Setting a specific date for a reunion will reinforce the fact with your child that he/she will see his/her older sibling again. This simple action can go a long way in creating a positive spirit regarding the situation.

4. Plan special family activities.
Give your child something to look forward to by planning special activities in which he/she can participate. A weekly pizza night, a trip to the zoo or ballpark, or a visit to an amusement park can stimulate enough enthusiasm to chase away the blues. If money is an issue, creativity can certainly help alleviate expenses.

Planning special activities with your younger child also represents a terrific opportunity for you to make memories with this future college bound student. Remember, it wasn't that long ago that your freshman was the same age as your kids at home are now.

5. Encourage contact.
Encourage regular phone calls and letter writing. Looking forward to talking with his/her big brother or sister on specific days can make your young child more accepting of the new situation. Perhaps you can persuade your young one to make his/her big sister a special present. Sad feelings can be diminished by energetically and dutifully working on a special project.

Encourage your freshman to take the time to drop a short note to his/her younger sibling. Send a roll of stamps and a box of stationary with your college student in order to impress upon him/her the importance of taking a few minutes to write. The length of the letter is not as important as the intent behind it.

Tips for you...
Undoubtedly, this will be a strange time for you as well. When your son or daughter leaves, you will inevitably feel a loss.

Countdown to College

For the last 18 years, you have hugged, encouraged, fed, yelled at, laughed with, tutored and enjoyed your kid. Things will now be different. The fact is, you will no longer be able to be there for him/her as you once were.

You have taken him/her to music lessons and soccer practices. You have comforted the trauma of a first pimple and have been scared out-of-your-wits watching him/her pull the car out of the driveway for the first time. Memories of good times shared seem brighter; memories of not so good times seem more trivial.

As you remember the past, don't forget to keep your eye on the future. *Not only can this be a time of exciting beginnings for your student, it can also be a time of exciting changes for you.* Now that you have a little more time on your hands, take inventory of your life and begin to do the things that you have put on hold.

1. Get to know your spouse again.

With one fewer kid at home, or even an empty nest, this is the perfect time to reintroduce yourself to your spouse. When families start to grow in size, spending time alone with your spouse becomes a luxury. Now that you have more time, plan dates as you did before you were married. Rekindle your friendship and your partnership.

2. Spend time on yourself.

What is it that you've wanted to do, but haven't had the time? Perhaps you can look into starting a new hobby or even go back to school and take a few classes. Now that your life is not organized around your student, your time is more freely yours to enjoy.

3. Spend time with others.

Due to having kids at home, you've probably not had time to cultivate friendships. With one fewer person vying for your time, now could be your chance. Call old friends or join a club. Volunteering for an organization could help you meet others who share your interests. Choose something that interests you and become involved!

4. Go to work.

Especially for empty nesters who regret not having worked while their children were at home, this is a perfect time to go back to your career. Do some research; call a few contacts; acquire the additional education and training that you need that will make you successful. It is never too late!

5. If you don't want to be tied down with a job that demands specific hours out of your day, consider being a home entrepreneur.

By reading money making magazines, you'll be introduced to a wide range of self-employment opportunities that require different levels of commitment and investment. There are so many different ways to make money and have fun while working from your home that you should be able to find something that is both intriguing and rewarding.

Practicing these principles will help you and your family make the emotional adjustments necessary to get through this difficult time. *Although the passing of time will always be a friend in helping get through tough days, taking a more aggressive role is usually best.*

<u>***Words to pass on...***</u>

"*T*here is nothing permanent except changes."
- Heraclitus, ancient Greek philosopher

"*T*he best portion of a good life is
the little nameless, unremembered
acts of kindness and love."
- William Wordsworth

***G*rowth is the process of**
responding positively to change.

39. Moving out:
what to send with your kid.

The week prior to the big move can definitely be crazy. With emotions running at peak levels, it's easy to overlook taking certain items that will be needed later. Taking the time to diligently pack things now will help your college student be more comfortable in his/her new home. It will also save your student money by not having to buy those items that he/she forgets to bring.

The following list will help keep you organized when the big moving day comes:

1.Personal items

travel iron	dental floss
laundry bag	aspirin
bathroom items	laundry detergent
razor	deodorant
shaving cream	hair comb/brush
shampoo	back pack
towels	first-aid kit
toothbrush	thermometer
toothpaste	Bible

Countdown to College

book of inspiration
address book
envelopes
postcards

stamps
easy recipes
laundry instructions

2. Desk items

desk lamp
waste basket
dictionary
thesaurus
quotation book
typewriter
calendars
notebooks
paper
paper clips
stapler

pens, pencils
highlighters
tape
scissors
ruler
envelopes
resource books
extension cord
calculator
correction fluid

3. Food items

can opener
mugs
plastic utensils
paper plates
electric pot
hair dryer

4. Comfort items

fan
mini fridge
popcorn maker
small stereo
tapes and CD's
athletic equipment

5. Room items

posters
decorations
personal pictures
pillows and cases
sheets

comforter
bed spread
alarm clock
telephone

6. Maintenance items

hammer	needle and trhead
screw driver	masking tape
wrench	thumb tacks

As easy as it is to forget to take some items, it is also easy to make the mistake of taking other items that are better off left at home. Here are a few items that could lead to roommate conflicts or space limitations:

7. Don't take

expensive jewelry	large stereo system
large pieces of furniture	too many clothes

A final note regarding your student's old room at home...

If possible, try to avoid converting your college student's room into an office, library or sewing room immediately upon his/her leaving for college. In this emotional time for your student, you could be pouring gasoline on the fire if you were to change the room over too soon.

After a few months pass and your student is enjoying college, bring up the idea of converting the room. Definitely talk about the subject before any action is taken. Of course if space limitations demand it, converting the old room into a bedroom for another sibling is understandable. Simple overcrowding makes it necessary, and your college student will certainly understand.

<u>*Words to pass on...*</u>

"*All* things change, nothing perishes."
- *Ovid, ancient Roman poet*

"*Let* our advance worrying become
advance thinking and planning."
—*Winston Churchill*

40. Paying for it all:
finding the money to pay for college.

For many parents, the thought of paying for college has been hanging over their heads for years...eighteen of them to be exact. *The American dream of sending your student to college can cost over $60,000.* Many private schools are more than 2 1/2 times that much. This amount doesn't even include books, transportation, and pizza money.

Pretty ominous, isn't it? Even more unnerving, college tuition will continue to increase.

Let's assume that the amount of money that you have been putting into the college fund the last few years is running on the short side. As you begin to add up the numbers, it becomes clear that your savings might be able to cover tuition...if for only one year. Before the stress knocks you off your feet, take a step back. All may not be lost.

The dilemma will get ugly, however, if you don't put it into high gear and immediately start looking into your options. Although there is no guarantee that you will be able to secure more money by starting earlier, you'll certainly have a better opportunity to take advantage of the huge financial aid market. *By educating yourself on the "ins-and-outs" of grants, scholarships, and loans, you will have a better chance of be-*

172

ing prepared to deal with the incredible costs associated with getting a higher education.

Here are a few areas that you would be wise to look into. *(Also, give strong consideration to ordering the Educational Assistance Council's College Aid Report. This individualized report is tailored to help your family solve the college funding questions.):*

1. Grants and scholarships...
✳ Federal grants...
Nothing beats free money! Although grants are predominantly based on family income and need, it is highly recommended that you look into the details of each program to see if you qualify. *Look into federal (and state) government grants, especially Pell Grants and SEOG/Supplemental Educational Opportunity Grants.* About 3.5 million students a year tap into this government gift program for a total of roughly $5.5 billion dollars. Have your student check with the Financial Aid office for other possibilities.

✳ Scholarships...
Scholarship hunting requires even more work, but the rewards are well worth it. *Corporations, private foundations, service clubs, and the college your student will be attending are all sources in which you and your student should look.* Although some scholarships are based on need, many are based on achievement. Ask the high school guidance counselor for help. Use library resources. Check into employer scholarship programs for children of employees. It doesn't matter if the scholarship is $100 or $1,000, check out every opportunity you find.

173

2. Low interest loans...

College loans are a fact of life. Very few students graduate from college without experiencing the realization that his/her student loans are now due. The good news is that most student loans have very low interest rates, and that means the pain of paying them back is somewhat softened.

✶ The government banker...

The Perkins Loan is the cheapest, but it is also the hardest federal loan to get. Having to pay no interest until after graduating (and then at an extremely low rate), it is usually reserved for lower income students. *Most students take out a Stafford Loan (the government pays the interest on the loan until the student graduates), and it is likely that your student will qualify for it as well.*

An important item to note is that most common student loans are issued through banks and other official lenders. *Some lenders charge origination fees that add to the cost of getting the loan, so it is a good idea to shop around in order to get the best deal.*

✶ The relative banker...

Sometimes, a wealthy relative volunteers to play the role of banker. If this scenario arises in your family, it's important to tread lightly. Borrowing money from family often seems like an easy thing to do; however, it potentially can be disastrous. You and your student should give this option a lot of thought before saying "yes."

3. Other alternatives...

Let's assume that your family doesn't qualify for a grant. It's probably a sure bet then that the $250 band scholarship and the student loan will not be enough to cover the college bill. In this case, withdrawing from the savings account becomes more of a necessity. If writing a check for the balance is a little difficult, there are other options:

✷ Considerations for your student...

Besides the obvious of getting a job in order to "take a little weight off mom and dad's shoulders," your student has a couple of ways he/she can help reduce college costs:

(1) Take advanced placement courses while in high school.

These courses allow a student the opportunity to skip a course in college for each course that is passed while in high school. By taking two Advanced Placement courses as a junior and two as a senior, your student can have up to 16 college credits before even starting college. This could be a few thousand dollars in tuition savings.

(2) Look into the College Work Study Program.

Administered through the Financial Aid office of the college or university, Work Study is available for students with unmet financial needs (tuition and room and board). The Financial Aid office finds students a job on campus, and the student works until the balance of the tuition is paid off.

(3) Save by picking up credits at the local community college during the summer.

Elective and introductory courses are often transferable which means the opportunity to pay community college rates for some classes and not major college rates. Summer school might not be something that your student will look forward to now, but when student loans start coming due

175

later, you can bet that your freshman will appreciate having experienced the inconvenience.

✳ Considerations for you...

Borrowing against your home or moonlighting with a part-time job are possibilities that you may want to consider in order to help you raise the money to pay for college. Depending on how strong your commitment is to pay for your son or daughter's schooling, these might be valid alternatives to consider. Only you can determine if the benefits of choosing these alternatives outweigh the costs that come with them.

Although college expenses can be staggering, the bottom line is that you do have options. By looking into all the possibilities, you have the chance of finding the fund sources that will work for your family. *Start your search early and leave no stone unturned.*

Words to pass on...

*"**M**oney...ranks with love as
man's greatest joy...
and it ranks with death as his
greatest source of anxiety."
- John Kenneth Galbraith*

***D**addy's little girl came home on semester break
and announced that she had decided on her life's
career."My English professor says I have a defi-
nite talent," she said. "He claims I can write for
money.""I agree," said her father. "In fact, that's
all you've done since you left for college."*

*"**F**or the resolute and detemined
there is time and opportunity."
—Ralph Waldo Emerson*

And finally...

As your children enter the college years, the road ahead will be a combination of exciting times and trying times. This guide has been written in order to help make the trying times a little smoother.

By melting emotional situations into working suggestions, *Countdown to College* is a guiding compass. It will provide suggestions that can help direct your response to tough situations. It will bring focus to certain problems that your son or daughter is likely to experience.

Parenting is a tough job, no doubt. Just because your college student is away at school, however, doesn't mean that you can breathe easier. In fact, the support that you provide to your son or daughter during this important transitional period could affect his or her future for years.

As your student becomes more independent, he/she will probably make a number of decisions that you will not agree with. It's sometimes difficult to know when to get involved and when to back off, but remember, learning from mistakes is a part of the maturation process. Make sure that you think about your actions and your words before you make the decision to get involved.

Countdown to College

Also, be careful to avoid attending college vicariously through your son or daughter. This is his/her time to experience and grow, not your time to live over. The decisions that will need to be made the next few years belong to your student. Be a source of support and guidance, yes, but make sure to give him/her room to develop into his/her own person.

Although you sometimes might wonder whether or not your son or daughter will ever get his/her act together, be patient. The chances are pretty darn good that your student will make it through this process. With your support during the tougher moments, your student will have an excellent chance of making the college years some of his or her most memorable years.

At the same time, your son or daughter's college years might even turn out to be a few of your proudest years. Enjoy them...

Countdown to College

Countdown to College

Countdown to College

OTHER TITLES FROM BLUE BIRD PUBLISHING

Available in bookstores and libraries.

Home Schools: An Alternative (4th ed)   *$12.95*
  A home schooling bestseller.
Home Education Resource Guide (4th e.) *$12.95*
  A home schooling bestseller.
Heartful Parenting   *$14.95*
  Discover the secret ingredient to successful parenting.
Dr. Christman's Learn-to-Read Book   *$15.95*
  Phonics program for all ages. Adopted by many
  literacy and right-to-read groups
Kindergarten at Home   *$22.95*
  An interactive kindergarten curriculum for
  homeschoolers. Useful activities for teachers too.
ADD to Excellent Without Drugs   *$12.95*
  A non-drug approach to helping children and adults
  with ADD/ ADHD.
Kids First! Family Education Program   *$12.95*
  Gets parents involved in their child's education.

More titles available on parenting & education.
Full catalog on Web Site: www.bluebird1.com

Blue Bird Publishing
2266 S. Dobson #275
Mesa AZ 85202
(602) 831-6063 FAX (602) 831-1829
Email: bluebird@bluebird1.com
Web Site: www.bluebird1.com